Talking Naturally and Confidently

Take It Easy!

Second Edition

Herman Bartelen

NATIONAL GEOGRAPHIC
LEARNING

Australia · Brazil · Mexico · Singapore · United Kingdom · United States

JN116667

Take It Easy! Second Edition—Talking Naturally and Confidently

Herman Bartelen

National Geographic Learning | Cengage Learning K.K.
No. 2 Funato Building 5th Floor
1-11-11 Kudankita, Chiyoda-ku
Tokyo 102-0073
Japan

Tel: 03-3511-4392
Fax: 03-3511-4391

Introduction

Take It Easy! is a low-intermediate textbook designed to help students develop both fluency and confidence as they aim to improve their English skills. This book has 12 thematic units which include functional and topic-based language, speaking and listening exercises, fluency-building activities, and a vocabulary bank for each unit. Each unit also contains a page for learning speaking strategies that will help students become more natural and confident speakers.

What's New in the Second Edition?

The second edition of *Take It Easy!* has been updated with improvements for both teachers and students. First, each unit has been revised and updated with activities and topics that reflect the concerns and lives of today's students. Second, there is a new review section for every three units. Each of these sections contains extra activities and a long listening section that can be used for either review or assessment purposes. Finally, the audio recordings have been updated to contain a larger variety of native speaker accents.

The First Page

Each unit begins with two conversational exchanges based on the language taught in the unit. These are followed by a substitution exercise that gets students speaking immediately and with ease.

Building Blocks

The Building Blocks sections include essential phrases and language that students will need in order to speak more fluently. These sections also include a listening exercise and a speaking activity for practicing the language and for building confidence.

Speaking Strategy

The Speaking Strategy section is designed to help students acquire language that will help them sound more natural. With the phrases from this section, students will be able to manipulate the unit's language points with more ease and confidence.

Wrap It Up

The final Wrap It Up section allows students to review and use the language from the whole unit. This section will allow students to consolidate what they have learned, and speak openly and freely.

Word Bank

The Word Bank is a list of useful phrases and words from the whole unit. Vocabulary development is considered an essential part of this textbook's approach to learning.

Take It Easy! aims to help students improve their speaking skills with fun and meaningful exercises that promote the learning of language and the friendly exchange of ideas, opinions, and experiences.

Good luck with your classes.

Herman Bartelen

Table of Contents

Unit	Title	Building Blocks 1
1	You and Me	Meeting and Greeting People
2	Growing Up	Past Tense Questions and Answers
3	At Home and at School	Expressing Frequency
	Review for Units 1–3	
4	Going Out	Talking about Future Plans
5	Food and Drink	Expressing Likes and Dislikes
6	The Future	Future Tense Questions and Answers
	Review for Units 4–6	
7	Travel	Talking about Location
8	Entertainment	Asking for and Giving Information
9	Staying Healthy	Describing Routines
	Review for Units 7–9	
10	People I Know	Describing People
11	Storytelling	Past Tense Questions and Answers
12	Society	Asking for and Giving Advice
	Review for Units 10–12	

How to Access the Audio Online

With a smartphone:

❶ Scan the QR code on the right to visit the website for the audio.

❷ Click the triangle (▶) to play each audio.

With a computer/PC:

❶ Visit the website below.
   https://ngljapan.com/tie2e-audio/

❷ Click the triangle (▶) to play each audio.

You and Me

Read the conversations with your partner. Then, make new conversations using the words in the boxes.

1
A: Hello.
B: Hi.
A: My name is Jim.
B: My name is Akemi. Nice to meet you.
A: Nice to meet you, too.
B: So, are you a student at this school?
A: Yeah, I'm an English major. What's your major?

your real name   your real name

2
A: Hey. How are you?
B: I'm okay. And you?
A: I'm fine. So, what do you want to do after school?
B: Let's go out for dinner.
A: Sounds good. Well, I have a class now. I have to go.
B: Okay. See you later.
A: Take it easy.

All right.   Bye.

Meeting and Greeting People

Look at the phrases for meeting and greeting people. Listen and repeat.

Greetings	Hi. Hey. Hello. Good morning. Good afternoon. Good evening. It's been a long time. Nice to meet you. I'm pleased to meet you.
Questions	How are you? How's it going? How are you doing? How about you? And you?
Answers to Greetings	I'm okay. Okay. Not bad. All right. Pretty good. I feel great. Fantastic. Not very good. I don't feel well. Terrible.
Saying Goodbye	Goodbye. Bye. See you later. Take care. Take it easy. It's been good talking to you. See you on Wednesday.

Listen In Listen to the conversations. Do the speakers know each other or not? Put the number of the conversation on the correct line.

A 03-06

Know each other _____   Are meeting for the first time _____

Speak Out Fill in the blanks with the words in the box. Use capitalization when necessary. Then, read the conversations with your partner.

1
A: Hello. Good _____.
B: Hi.
A: Let me _____ myself. My name is John.
B: I'm Sally. _____ to meet you.
A: I'm _____ to meet you, too.

you	sounds	afternoon
bye	pleased	introduce
nice	how	so

2
A: Hey. _____ are you doing?
B: Fantastic. And _____?
A: I'm okay. _____, what do you want to do tonight?
B: Let's go out for dinner.
A: _____ good. See you after school then.
B: _____.

Hesitating

When you are not sure what to say or you are looking for something to say, you can use phrases for hesitating. Listen and repeat.

> • Well, …   • um …   • ah …   • Let me see.   • Anyway, …

 **Fill in the blanks. Then, read the sentences to your partner.**

Hi. My name is _____.

Let me … um … introduce myself … Well,

I was … ah … born in _____

and I now live in _____.

Let me see. My major at school is

_____. I think I'm a good

student and I love to speak English.

Um … in my free time, I like to

_____.

Anyway, nice to meet you.

Speak Out 2   **Ask your partner the questions. Use phrases for hesitating when you answer.**

1. So, where do you live now?   ⇒ Now? Well, I live in …
2. Do you live by yourself or with your family?   ⇒ Um … I …
3. What do your parents do?   ⇒ Well, my father is a …
4. So, what do your brothers and sisters do?   ⇒ Well, …
5. Do you have any pets?   ⇒ Ah …
6. What is your major at school?   ⇒ My major at school is … ah …
7. What is your favorite subject at school?   ⇒ My favorite subject at school is … um …
8. So, do you like studying English?   ⇒ Do I like studying English? Well, …
9. Do you spend a lot of time with your friends?   ⇒ Well, …
10. What do you usually do in your free time?   ⇒ Let me see. Um … in my free time, I like to …

Present Tense Questions and Answers

Look at the present tense questions and answers. Listen and repeat.

Are you from Okinawa?	→ Yes, I am. / No, I'm not. I'm from Tokyo.
Is your teacher Canadian?	→ Yes, he is. / No, he isn't. He's Australian.
Do they study Korean?	→ Yes, they do. / No, they don't. They study English.
Does your brother live at home?	→ Yes, he does. / No, he doesn't. He lives by himself.
Who is your best friend?	→ My best friend is John.
What are your favorite subjects?	→ My favorite subjects are science and history.
Where do you usually eat?	→ I usually eat at home.
When do we have a test?	→ We have a test on Friday.
Why do you study English?	→ I think it's a useful language to know.

 **Listen to the questions and complete the answers.**

1. _____, she's British.   2. No, they _____ from Ireland.   3. I _____ to play sports.

4. Yeah, she _____.   5. We have _____ study in the library.   6. No, _____ _____ Wednesday.

 **Fill in the blanks with the words in the box. Then, ask your partner the questions. Use phrases for hesitating when you answer.**

Do   Does   Is   Are   Why   When   Where   Who   What

1. _____ subjects do you like best at school?

2. _____ your father or mother speak English?

3. _____ is English useful?

4. _____ do you have English classes?

5. _____ do you live now?

6. _____ you like to study?

7. _____ your English teacher American?

8. _____ do you spend a lot of time with?

9. _____ your parents from this area?

WRAP IT UP

Write your answers to the questions. Then, ask your partner the questions. When answering, use the questions "And you?" and "How about you?"

Example   **A:** Do you live with your family?
B: Yes, I do. We live in Tokyo. How about you?
A: I live by myself in Yokohama.

Questions	Your answers	Your partner's answers
1. Do you live with your family?		
2. Where do you live?		
3. Do you like where you live?		
4. What does everyone in your family do?		
5. Does anyone in your family speak English?		
6. Do you live near any of your relatives?		
7. Is this school far from your home?		
8. What subjects do you like studying at school?		
9. What do you like and dislike about school?		
10. Do you have a part-time job?		
11. What do you like to do in your free time?		
12. Who do you spend a lot of time with?		
13. When is your birthday?		

Word Bank

Check (✔) the words that you know. If there are any words that you don't know, look them up in your dictionary.

Useful Phrases

- [ ] Take it easy.
- [ ] See you later.
- [ ] Sounds good.
- [ ] Pretty good.
- [ ] Yeah.
- [ ] How about you?
- [ ] And you?
- [ ] Anyway, …
- [ ] Well, …
- [ ] So, …
- [ ] by the way
- [ ] in my free time
- [ ] around here

Nouns

- [ ] Monday
- [ ] Tuesday
- [ ] Wednesday
- [ ] Thursday
- [ ] Friday
- [ ] Saturday
- [ ] Sunday
- [ ] today
- [ ] morning
- [ ] afternoon
- [ ] evening
- [ ] breakfast
- [ ] lunch
- [ ] dinner
- [ ] supper
- [ ] family
- [ ] parents
- [ ] father
- [ ] mother

- [ ] brother
- [ ] sister
- [ ] grandfather
- [ ] grandmother
- [ ] grandchild
- [ ] relative
- [ ] uncle
- [ ] aunt
- [ ] cousin
- [ ] nephew
- [ ] niece
- [ ] everyone
- [ ] best friend
- [ ] classmate
- [ ] student
- [ ] home
- [ ] apartment
- [ ] train station
- [ ] area
- [ ] building
- [ ] library
- [ ] school
- [ ] period
- [ ] subject
- [ ] major
- [ ] Korean

Verbs

- [ ] be born
- [ ] be in a hurry
- [ ] live
- [ ] live by *oneself*
- [ ] have
- [ ] have a test
- [ ] have a part-time job
- [ ] do

- [ ] want to do *something*
- [ ] ride *one's* bike
- [ ] buy
- [ ] go out
- [ ] cook
- [ ] study
- [ ] work
- [ ] complete
- [ ] meet
- [ ] greet
- [ ] introduce
- [ ] hesitate
- [ ] spend time with *someone*
- [ ] love
- [ ] like
- [ ] dislike

Adjectives

- [ ] American
- [ ] Australian
- [ ] British
- [ ] Canadian
- [ ] English
- [ ] European
- [ ] Irish
- [ ] New Zealand
- [ ] Scottish
- [ ] Welsh
- [ ] useful
- [ ] nice

Adverbs and Prepositions

- [ ] near
- [ ] close to
- [ ] usually

Growing Up

I used to be like you when I was young.

Really?

Read the conversations with your partner. Then, make new conversations using the words in the boxes.

A: What kind of music did you listen to in junior high school?

B: I listened to a lot of rock music.

A: Really?

B: Yeah. My parents used to play it at home.

A: Did you listen to pop music, too?

B: No, not very much. How about you?

A: I used to listen to pop music all the time.

high school   jazz   older brother
elementary school   Disney younger sister

A: When I was six years old, I broke my arm.

B: Really?

A: I was climbing a tree and I fell down.

B: Did you cry?

A: Definitely. It hurt a lot. Have you ever broken any bones?

B: No, but I had a lot of bicycle accidents when I was younger.

leg   riding my bicycle
thumb   standing on a chair

13

Past Tense Questions and Answers

Look at the past tense questions and answers. Listen and repeat.

Were your high school classes interesting?	→ Yes, they were. / No, they weren't.
Was your high school far from your home?	→ Yes, it was. / No, it wasn't.
Did your family live in an apartment?	→ Yes, we did. / No, we didn't. We lived in a house.
Who was your best friend in high school?	→ My best friend was Ayako.
What did you usually do after school?	→ After school, I usually played outside.
Where did you go for your school trip?	→ We went to Kyoto for our school trip.
When did you graduate from high school?	→ I graduated in March last year.
Why did you join the music club?	→ I joined because I wanted to learn to play drums.

Listen In **Listen to the conversations and complete the sentences.**

1. Tom _____ up in the countryside, and he always played _____ with his _____.

2. Lisa _____ all subjects in _____ school, but she was not very good at _____.

3. Alex was _____ in Osaka, but he _____ in New York City for _____ years.

 **Speak Out** **Fill in the blanks with the words in the box. Then, ask your partner the questions. Always answer with at least two sentences.**

1. What _____ your favorite food as a child?

2. _____ you grow up in the countryside or the city?

3. _____ you good at any sports at school?

4. Where _____ your high school?

5. Who _____ you hang out with in high school?

6. When _____ you get your first smartphone?

7. Who _____ your good neighborhood friends?

8. What _____ you usually do after school?

9. _____ you dye your hair when you were in high school?

10. _____ you have to wear a school uniform?

did	were	was

Speaking Strategy

Showing Interest

When you want to keep a conversation going, you can use phrases for showing interest and follow-up questions. Listen and repeat.

Showing Interest	• Really? • That's interesting. • Wow! • You're kidding!
Follow-Up Questions	• Why? • How come? • How was it? • Do you still do that?

 **Speak Out 1** Fill in the blanks. Then, read the conversations with your partner.

1
A: When I was in high school, I played on the volleyball team.
B: _____ How was it?
A: It was fun.

2
A: I loved visiting my grandparents when I was a child.
B: _____ Why?
A: Because they gave me sweets all the time.

3
A: When I was a junior high school student, I used to play in a band.
B: _____ Do you still do that?
A: No. I quit playing.

Speak Out 2 Circle the correct one for your childhood. Then, read the sentences to your partner. Use phrases for showing interest and follow-up questions when you respond.

1. When I was six years old, I [could / couldn't] use chopsticks.
2. Our family [traveled / didn't travel] a lot together when I was in elementary school.
3. When I was a child, I [thought / didn't think] Japanese was very difficult.
4. I [liked / didn't like] eating rice when I was a small kid.
5. My friends and I [played / didn't play] hide and seek a lot.
6. I [loved / didn't love] reading comic books when I was younger.
7. When I was in kindergarten, I [could / couldn't] put on my clothes by myself.
8. I [used to / didn't use to] go to bed around 8:00 when I was a child.
9. When I was in elementary school, I [went / didn't go] camping very often.

Talking about the Past

Look at the questions and answers for talking about the past. Listen and repeat.

- Have you ever gone camping? → Yes, I have. I went three weeks ago. / No, I haven't.
- Did you use to watch TV a lot? → Yes, I did. / No, I didn't. I used to read a lot of books.
- What did you use to do after school? → I used to play outside.
- Where were you living? → I was living in Chiba at the time.

Listen In Listen to the conversations and complete the sentences.

1. The man _____ _____ play baseball with his friends every _____. Their mothers used to _____ _____ for them.

2. When the man was young, he _____ basketball, and he always used to _____ it on TV. His father used to _____ him to basketball games.

3. The woman and her _____ used to _____ _____ music when she was a _____ _____ student. Her friends came over to her house and they _____.

4. The man once _____ Mt. Fuji when he was in high school. The woman's family used to ____ _____, but they _____ _____ Mt. Fuji.

 **Speak Out** Ask your partner the questions. Make some comments after you answer "Yes." or "No."

1. Have you ever traveled abroad?
2. Have you ever lost your phone?
3. Have you ever gone hiking?
4. Where were you living when you were in junior high school?
5. Did you use to collect anything?
6. Did you use to travel in Japan with your family?
7. Did you use to watch a lot of animation?
8. Did you use to play outside a lot?
9. What did you use to do on the weekends?
10. What did you use to do during the summer holidays?

WRAP IT UP

Write your answers to the questions. Then, ask your partner the questions. Use phrases for showing interest and follow-up questions when you answer.

Example
A: What do you remember about being very young?
B: I remember that my older sister and I used to draw pictures all the time.
A: That's interesting. Do you still like drawing pictures?
B: Yes, I do. I always carry my sketchbook when I go out.

Questions	Your answers	Your partner's answers
1. What do you remember about being very young?		
2. What did you like to do when you were small?		
3. What kind of food and drinks did you use to like as a child?		
4. Did you enjoy elementary school?		
5. What subjects did you like when you were in junior high school?		
6. What did you use to do during winter holidays?		
7. What are your good memories from growing up?		
8. Who were the important people to you in high school?		
9. Did you play video games very often?		
10. What have been the big events in your life so far?		

Word Bank

Check (✔) the words that you know. If there are any words that you don't know, look them up in your dictionary.

Useful Phrases

- [ ] when I was younger
- [ ] when I was six years old
- [ ] at the time
- [ ] so far
- [ ] for 14 years
- [ ] all the time
- [ ] every summer
- [ ] every weekend
- [ ] after school
- [ ] at home

Nouns

- [ ] kindergarten
- [ ] elementary school
- [ ] junior high school
- [ ] high school
- [ ] memory
- [ ] summer holiday
- [ ] school trip
- [ ] subject
- [ ] interest
- [ ] volleyball
- [ ] baseball
- [ ] basketball
- [ ] sketchbook
- [ ] comic book
- [ ] city
- [ ] countryside
- [ ] rice field
- [ ] chopsticks
- [ ] sweets
- [ ] finger
- [ ] thumb

Verbs

- [ ] be born
- [ ] grow up
- [ ] graduate from
- [ ] get married
- [ ] live with *someone*
- [ ] be good at *something*
- [ ] be bad at *something*
- [ ] remember
- [ ] enjoy
- [ ] collect *something*
- [ ] listen to music
- [ ] play music
- [ ] play in a band
- [ ] play *one's* CD
- [ ] dye *one's* hair
- [ ] fall asleep
- [ ] go to bed
- [ ] put on clothes
- [ ] make lunch
- [ ] cook
- [ ] read
- [ ] draw
- [ ] dance
- [ ] carry
- [ ] travel
- [ ] travel abroad
- [ ] go camping
- [ ] go hiking
- [ ] go out
- [ ] come over
- [ ] give *someone something*
- [ ] take *someone* to *a place or activity*
- [ ] hang out with *someone*
- [ ] play hide and seek

- [ ] climb a tree
- [ ] ride a bicycle
- [ ] have an accident
- [ ] fall down
- [ ] break an arm
- [ ] break a bone
- [ ] cry
- [ ] hurt
- [ ] quit

Adjectives

- [ ] beautiful
- [ ] cute
- [ ] fun
- [ ] boring
- [ ] easy
- [ ] difficult
- [ ] important
- [ ] unimportant
- [ ] favorite
- [ ] loud
- [ ] quiet

Adverbs and Prepositions

- [ ] especially
- [ ] inside
- [ ] outside
- [ ] early
- [ ] late

How often do you eat at home?

Never. I'm a street cat.

Read the conversations with your partner. Then, make new conversations using the words in the boxes.

1

A: Guess what. I bought a TV for my room.

B: That's great! So, how often do you watch TV?

A: About four hours a day.

B: Really? That's a lot of time. What do you usually watch?

A: I almost always watch British comedy shows. How about you?

B: Actually, I don't watch TV very often.

Wow!   American crime shows
rarely watch TV

You're kidding.   Japanese variety shows
hardly ever watch TV

2

A: What are you doing?

B: I'm studying.

A: Really? So, how often do you study?

B: I study at home every day. And you?

A: I study once or twice a week.

B: Do you know that we have a vocabulary test today?

A: Oh no! That's terrible. I forgot to study.

night   two or three times
You're kidding!

weekend   three evenings
I didn't know that.

Expressing Frequency

Look at the questions and answers for expressing frequency. Listen and repeat.

What do you usually do in the mornings?	→ I always take a shower and then eat breakfast.
What do you usually do after school?	→ I almost always go straight home.
What do you do on the weekends?	→ I often sleep in late.
What do you do on Saturdays?	→ I usually hang out with my friends.
What do you do in the evenings?	→ I sometimes play music.
Do you often study in the library?	→ No, I don't study in the library very often.
Do you study a lot during the week?	→ I rarely study during the week.
Do you cook for your family very often?	→ I hardly ever cook for my family.
How often do you iron your clothes?	→ I never iron my clothes.
How often do you put out the garbage?	→ I put it out every Friday.
How often do you do the laundry?	→ It depends, but I usually do it twice a week.

Listen In   **Listen to the conversations and circle the phrases that you hear.**

1. always / almost always / often / usually / sometimes / not … very often / rarely / hardly ever / never
2. always / almost always / often / usually / sometimes / not … very often / rarely / hardly ever / never
3. always / almost always / often / usually / sometimes / not … very often / rarely / hardly ever / never
4. always / almost always / often / usually / sometimes / not … very often / rarely / hardly ever / never

 **Ask your partner the questions. Always answer with at least two sentences.**

1. How often do you study in the library?
2. What do you usually do after school?
3. How many times a week do you exercise?
4. Do you play video games very often?
5. What do you usually do in the mornings?
6. Do you go for a walk sometimes?
7. How often do you put out the garbage?
8. What do you usually do on the weekends?

Speaking Strategy

Talking about Personal News

When you introduce news, you need to get attention from the listener. When you hear the news, you need to use phrases for responding. Listen and repeat. A/25

Introducing News	• Guess what! • Did I tell you what happened?
Responding to News	• Really? • Wow! • That's fantastic! • That's great! • You're kidding! • I didn't know that. • Oh no! • That's terrible. • That's too bad.
Asking Questions	• What are you doing? • Why is that? • Why? • Who? • What? • Where? • When?
Giving Reasons	• I'm studying because I have a test. • I have a test so I'm studying.

 **Speak Out 1** **Fill in the blanks. Then, read the conversations with your partner.**

1
A: _____ you doing?
B: I'm playing a new video game.
A: _____! So, _____ did you get it?

2
A: _____ what! The school has a new English conversation lounge.
B: _____. Why?
A: They built it _____ students can practice English more.

3
A: Did I tell you what happened? I bought a computer last week but it's already broken.
B: _____. So, _____ are you going to do?
A: I'm going to ask for my money back _____ it's still new.

Speak Out 2 **Read the sentences to your partner. Use phrases for responding to news and follow-up questions when you respond.**

1. Guess what! I got 700 on the TOEIC test.
2. Did I tell you about our new teacher? He never gives us homework.
3. Do you know that Miki and Bob are dating now?
4. Guess what! I missed the test this morning.
5. Did I tell you what happened yesterday? I lost my room key.
6. Do you know that our teacher used to be a news reporter?

Using "How …?" Questions

Look at the questions using "How" and the answers. Listen and repeat.

How do you get to school every day?	→ I ride my bike.
How many times a week do you have English classes?	→ I have English classes twice a week.
How often do you use social media?	→ I use social media every day.
How long does it take you to get to school?	→ It takes about one hour.
How much housework do you do every week?	→ I don't do housework.
How many students are there in this school?	→ There are about 1,600 students.
How much does it cost to go to a movie nowadays?	→ It costs about 2,000 yen.
How big is your room?	→ It's small.

 **Listen to the conversations and answer the questions.**

1. How often does the man clean his room? _____
2. How long does it take the man to get to the station? _____
3. How much does it cost for a ticket to a soccer game? _____
4. How much homework does the class have to do every week? _____

 **Ask your partner the questions.**

1. How often do you clean your room?
2. How long does it take you to clean your room?
3. How many minutes does it take you to walk to the nearest train station?
4. How much homework do you do every week?
5. How often do you do the dishes every week?
6. How much money do you spend every month?
7. How many students are there in this class?
8. How big is your hometown?
9. How long do you usually sleep on the weekends?
10. How many days a week do you go to school?

WRAP IT UP

Complete the questions. Then, ask your partner the questions. Use phrases for responding to news and follow-up questions when you answer.

Example   **A:** How often do you have dinner at home?
B: I always have dinner at home.
A: Wow! Does your mother cook for you every day?
B: Yeah, but my father sometimes cooks on the weekends.

Questions	Your partner's answers
1. How often do you _____ _____?	
2. What do you usually do _____ _____?	
3. How long does it take you to _____ _____?	
4. How much does it cost for _____ _____?	
5. How many days a month do you _____ _____?	
6. Do you usually eat _____ _____?	
7. Do you sometimes go to _____ _____?	
8. How far is it from _____ to _____?	
9. How many _____ do you have?	
10. How big is _____ _____?	

Word Bank

Check (✔) the words that you know. If there are any words that you don't know, look them up in your dictionary.

Useful Phrases

- [ ] Guess what!
- [ ] It depends.
- [ ] Really?
- [ ] Wow!
- [ ] That's fantastic!
- [ ] That's great!
- [ ] You're kidding.
- [ ] That's too bad!
- [ ] That's terrible.
- [ ] Oh no!
- [ ] How much does it cost?
- [ ] Actually, …
- [ ] Anyway, …
- [ ] at home
- [ ] at school
- [ ] six hours a day
- [ ] once a week
- [ ] twice a month
- [ ] three times a year
- [ ] in the mornings
- [ ] in the evenings
- [ ] on Mondays
- [ ] every Friday
- [ ] every day
- [ ] on purpose
- [ ] nowadays
- [ ] these days

Nouns

- [ ] hometown
- [ ] mom
- [ ] dad
- [ ] room key
- [ ] motorbike

- [ ] gym
- [ ] game
- [ ] ticket
- [ ] crime show
- [ ] comedy show
- [ ] variety show
- [ ] news
- [ ] news reporter
- [ ] frequency
- [ ] social media

Verbs

- [ ] be over
- [ ] finish
- [ ] express
- [ ] respond
- [ ] forget
- [ ] miss
- [ ] lose
- [ ] steal
- [ ] take
- [ ] ride a bike
- [ ] walk to the station
- [ ] get to school
- [ ] go home
- [ ] do housework
- [ ] do the laundry
- [ ] do the dishes
- [ ] iron
- [ ] clean *one's* room
- [ ] put out the garbage
- [ ] cook for *someone*
- [ ] eat breakfast
- [ ] take a shower
- [ ] wash *one's* hair
- [ ] sleep in late

- [ ] play music
- [ ] play a video game
- [ ] go for a walk
- [ ] hang out with *someone*
- [ ] date
- [ ] work out
- [ ] buy
- [ ] spend money
- [ ] cost 2,000 yen
- [ ] cost 30 dollars
- [ ] cost for *something*
- [ ] work at a part-time job
- [ ] study abroad
- [ ] get 700 on the TOEIC test

Adjectives

- [ ] American
- [ ] British
- [ ] Japanese
- [ ] small
- [ ] big
- [ ] cheap
- [ ] expensive
- [ ] busy

Adverbs and Prepositions

- [ ] always
- [ ] almost always
- [ ] often
- [ ] usually
- [ ] sometimes
- [ ] not … very often
- [ ] rarely
- [ ] hardly ever
- [ ] never

Speak Out 1 Fill in the blanks with the words in the boxes. Use capitalization when necessary. Then, read the conversations with your partner.

1

A: Hi.

B: _____. _____ are you doing?

A: _____ good.

B: _____ you from around here?

A: _____, I go to school here. I'm Jim, _____ the way.

B: Hi, Jim. My _____ is Emiko.

A: Hi, Emiko. _____, what do you study?

B: I'm an English major.

yes hello pretty how by are name so

2

A: So, where did you _____ up, Mari?

B: I _____ up in the city. It was small but there were some parks.

A: _____ nice. Did you like it?

B: Oh, yeah. It was _____. My friends and I always played in the park or at school. _____ about you?

A: I was born in Nagasaki, but I grew _____ in Shizuoka. My father _____ born there.

B: That's interesting. _____ you like it?

A: Yeah, my friends and I _____ to _____ swimming in the summer time and skiing in the winter.

B: _____? That sounds great. Do you _____ ski?

A: Of course.

up go sounds really grow fun did how was used grew still

3

A: _____ do you _____ do after school?

B: I _____ go to the gym.

A: That's great! How _____ do you go?

B: I always go on Tuesdays and Wednesdays. I also _____ a part-time job.

A: How often do you work?

B: Just _____ a week. How _____ you? _____ you have a part-time job?

A: Yeah, I work _____ Friday and Saturday at a pastry shop.

B: You're _____! That's a great job.

do   usually   kidding   have   sometimes   twice   often   every   what   about

🔊 **Speak Out 2**   **Talk about one of the topics. Keep the talk going for at least 1 minute.**

your family	your friends	your best friends in elementary school

music you liked when younger	your school	your high school English teachers

travel abroad	camping	your morning routine

your weekend routine	your housework	your grandparents

🔊 **Speak Out 3**   **Fill in the blanks with the words in the box. Then, ask your partner the questions. Always answer with at least two sentences and continue the conversation with follow-up questions.**

1. So, where _____ you live now?

2. What _____ you do in your free time now?

3. What _____ your favorite subjects at school now?

4. _____ you like where you live? Why or why not?

5. _____ you have a part-time job now?

6. What kind of music _____ you listen to when you were young?

7. What _____ you usually do after school when you were a junior high or high school student?

8. What _____ some of your favorite foods as a child?

9. _____ Disney important to you as a child?

10. What _____ you use to do during the summer holidays?

11. What _____ you usually do after school now?

12. Recently, how often _____ you exercise?

---

do   did   are   were   was

 *Speak Out 4*   **Ask your partner the questions. Always answer with at least two sentences and continue the conversation with follow-up questions.**

1. Where do you live now?
2. Do you like where you live? Why or why not?
3. What do you like to do in your free time?
4. What do you love about school?
5. Did you play a lot of sports at school?
6. Could you use chopsticks when you were five years old?
7. What time did you usually wake up and go to bed when you were a child?
8. Did your family travel a lot together when you were young?
9. Did you think studying Japanese was very difficult?
10. What did you use to do during the winter holidays?
11. What were your favorite subjects at school?
12. How often do you watch TV?
13. How often do you study?
14. How many days a week do you exercise?
15. Have you ever traveled abroad?

 **Listen In 1** **Listen to the conversations and answer the questions.** A 31-36

1. **a)** Where are the two people? _____

   b) Do they know each other? _____

2. **a)** How does the man feel? _____

   b) Why couldn't the man study for the test? _____

3. **a)** Where was the woman born? _____

   b) How long did the woman live in Osaka? _____

4. **a)** How many times has the man been to Hong Kong? _____

   b) What happened on the man's school trip? _____

5. **a)** What two things will the woman do after school? _____

   b) Who never studies in the library, the man or the woman? _____

6. **a)** When and what are the family going to do? _____

   b) How much is the ticket? _____

 Listen In 2 **Listen to the conversations and read the statements. Circle T for true and F for false. Correct the false statements.** A 37-42

1. **a)** The people know each other. T / F

   b) They will meet on Friday. T / F

2. **a)** The man grew up in Gumma Prefecture. T / F

   b) The man lived in Tokyo for 14 years. T / F

3. **a)** The woman belonged to the brass band club and volleyball club in high school. T / F

   b) The woman belonged to the volleyball club for three years. T / F

4. **a)** Both of the speakers played soccer when they were young. T / F

   b) Both of the speakers have seen a professional soccer game. T / F

5. **a)** Both of the speakers have history homework every week. T / F

   b) The woman's teacher gives one hour of homework every week. T / F

6. **a)** The speaker often meets his friends during the week. T / F

   b) The speaker and his friends do their homework together at school. T / F

Going Out

What do you want to do tonight?

Let's go out and chase some zebra.

Read the conversations with your partner. Then, make new conversations using the words in the boxes.

1

A: What are you going to do tomorrow?

B: I plan to see a movie. How about you?

A: I'm going to visit some friends and play video games.

B: Do you want to meet for dinner in the evening?

A: That's a good idea. Where do you want to meet?

B: How about meeting in front of the station at 6 o'clock?

A: Sounds fine.

B: Okay. I'll see you at 6:00.

study	play soccer	at the school

work out	hang out	at your house

2

A: So, how was your weekend?

B: It was good.

A: What did you do on Saturday?

B: In the morning, I slept in and then I cleaned my room.

A: How about in the afternoon?

B: I went out to have lunch with my friends.

A: How was it?

B: It was fun.

great	watched some surfing videos
play table tennis	

not bad	did some homework
go shopping	

Talking about Future Plans

Look at the questions and answers for talking about future plans. Listen and repeat.

What are you going to do tonight?	→ I'm going to study for a test.
Where are you going to go?	→ We're going to go to a neighborhood shop.
What are your plans for the weekend?	→ I plan to go shopping with my friends.
What do you want to do tonight?	→ I want to sing karaoke.
Do you feel like going to a movie?	→ I'd love to but I'm busy.
Let's go out for dinner on Saturday.	→ Okay. That's a good idea.
Do you want to go for a coffee?	→ Sure. That sounds good.
Where do you want to meet?	→ Let's meet at the station.
What time shall we meet?	→ How about 6 o'clock?
I want to confirm that.	→ It's the 21st at 2:00 in the afternoon.

 Listen to the conversations and fill in the blanks.

What will they do?	**Where will they meet?**	**When and what time will they meet?**
1. go bowling	_____	_____
2. _____	at the _____ of the stadium	_____
3. _____	_____	_____

 Fill in the blanks with the words in the box. Use capitalization when necessary. Then, read the conversations with your partner.

1
A: What do you _____ to do on Saturday, the 11th?

B: How about _____ to a show?

A: That _____ good. Where and what time shall we meet?

B: Well, _____ meet at the mall at 5:00.

let's	to do	going
feel	want	meet
plans	sounds	

2
A: What are your _____ for the weekend?

B: Nothing much. Do you want _____ something?

A: I'd love to. Do you _____ like going to the park to play frisbee?

B: Okay. Let's _____ at the park at noon.

Asking Follow-Up Questions

Asking follow-up questions is a good way to keep a conversation going. Listen and repeat.

A 47

- What are you going to do tomorrow? → I'm going skateboarding.
- Who are you going with? → I'm going with a friend.
- Where are you going? → We're going to a local park.
- When are you going? → We're planning to go in the afternoon.
- Why do you like skateboarding? → I like it because it's so much fun.
- When did you start skateboarding? → I started when I was around eight years old.
- Was it difficult at the beginning? → Yes, it was very difficult.
- Are skateboards expensive? → It depends.

 **Speak Out 1**   **Write two follow-up questions for each conversation. Then, read the conversations with your partner.**

1 **A:** What are you doing next Saturday?

　　B: I'm planning to go swimming.

　　A: _____

2 **A:** My family is planning to go camping on the weekend.

　　B: _____

3 **A:** On Sunday, I'm going to Disneyland.

　　B: _____

 **Speak Out 2**   **Ask your partner the questions. Then, continue the conversation with follow-up questions.**

1. What are your plans for the weekend?
2. What are you going to do tomorrow night?
3. What are you planning for the next vacation?
4. What are you doing tonight after school?
5. Do you have any plans for next month?

Talking about Past Activities

Look at the questions and answers for talking about past activities. Listen and repeat. A 48

What did you do last night?	→ I went out with my friends and then we had dinner.
How was it?	→ It was great.
What did you do on Monday the 21st?	→ I slept until noon. Then, I worked out in the afternoon.
Who did you go with?	→ I went with some of my classmates.
Where did you go on the weekend?	→ We went to a park near my home.
When did you get back home?	→ We got back home around 10:00.

Questions   How was Tuesday?   How was your week?   How was your weekend?
How was it?   Did you have fun?   Was it good?

Answers   Okay.   It was okay.   It wasn't bad.   It was all right.   It was good.
It was interesting.   It was great.   Wonderful.   Fantastic.   It was relaxing.
It was dull.   It was boring.   It wasn't so good.   It was terrible.
It was quiet.   It was busy.

 **Listen In**   Listen to the conversations and fill in the blanks. A 49-51

Activity 1	Activity 2	Activity 3
1. _____	went _____ with _____	tried horseback riding
2. _____	went _____ with _____	went to see _____
3. _____	went _____ with _____	_____

 **Speak Out**   Ask your partner the questions.
Make follow-up questions.

1. What did you do last Monday evening?
2. What did you do this morning?
3. What did you do on the 27th?
4. What did you do Friday night?
5. How was yesterday?
6. How was your weekend?

WRAP IT UP 1

Suppose today is the 1st. Make your schedule for: studying, working out, meeting friends, and watching a film. Then, make plans with your partner to: go to a concert, go to the beach, go shopping, and go to an aquarium. Walk around the class and talk to as many classmates as possible.

Example
A: Do you want to go to a concert on Sunday, the 12th?
B: I'd love to but I have to study on Sunday because I have an exam on Monday.
A: Okay. How about Friday, the 10th?
B: That's fine. What time does the concert start?
A: It starts at 6:30. Where and what time shall we meet?
B: Well, let's meet at 6:00 in front of the station.
A: Okay. I'll see you at 6:00 on the 10th.

Sunday	Monday	Tuesday	Wednesday	Thursday	Friday	Saturday
			1 Today	2	3	4
5	6	7	8	9	10	11
12 studying	13	14	15	16	17	18
19	20	21	22	23	24	25

WRAP IT UP 2

Role-play in pairs. Pretend that you did the things you planned. Ask and talk about the events. Ask follow-up questions.

Word Bank

Check (✔) the words that you know. If there are any words that you don't know, look them up in your dictionary.

Useful Phrases

- [ ] Bye for now.
- [ ] Of course.
- [ ] Sure.
- [ ] That's fine.
- [ ] Sounds fine.
- [ ] Cool.
- [ ] If you have the chance, …
- [ ] during the week
- [ ] on the weekend
- [ ] on the 21st
- [ ] on Friday
- [ ] in the morning
- [ ] at noon
- [ ] in the afternoon
- [ ] in the evening
- [ ] at night
- [ ] at 6:00
- [ ] at 6 o'clock
- [ ] last week
- [ ] last Monday evening
- [ ] the day before yesterday
- [ ] last night
- [ ] this morning
- [ ] tonight
- [ ] tomorrow morning
- [ ] tomorrow night
- [ ] the day after tomorrow
- [ ] next week
- [ ] It depends.

Nouns

- [ ] invitation
- [ ] preference
- [ ] hot spring
- [ ] amusement park
- [ ] stadium
- [ ] gate
- [ ] zoo
- [ ] zebra

Verbs

- [ ] suppose
- [ ] try
- [ ] chase
- [ ] invite
- [ ] meet
- [ ] be in good shape
- [ ] be in bad shape
- [ ] look tired
- [ ] take it easy
- [ ] sleep in
- [ ] stay overnight
- [ ] feel like doing *something*
- [ ] prefer to do *something*
- [ ] do *one's* schoolwork
- [ ] clean *one's* room
- [ ] watch TV
- [ ] get something to eat
- [ ] have lunch
- [ ] have dinner
- [ ] have a date
- [ ] go bowling
- [ ] go dancing
- [ ] go fishing
- [ ] go hiking
- [ ] go horseback riding
- [ ] go shopping
- [ ] go for a drive
- [ ] go to the beach
- [ ] catch a movie
- [ ] see a movie
- [ ] see a play
- [ ] play tennis

Adjectives

- [ ] French
- [ ] Italian
- [ ] Thai
- [ ] wonderful
- [ ] fantastic
- [ ] great
- [ ] not bad
- [ ] okay
- [ ] all right
- [ ] interesting
- [ ] exciting
- [ ] fancy
- [ ] beautiful
- [ ] relaxing
- [ ] comfortable
- [ ] quiet
- [ ] busy
- [ ] easy
- [ ] difficult
- [ ] tough
- [ ] tired
- [ ] dull
- [ ] boring
- [ ] bad
- [ ] terrible
- [ ] uncomfortable

Adverbs and Prepositions

- [ ] in front of
- [ ] until

Food and Drink

Read the conversations with your partner. Then, make new conversations using the words in the boxes.

A: What kind of food do you like?
B: I love Japanese food, but I can't stand sushi.
A: That's unusual. So, what are your favorite dishes?
B: I like tofu and noodles.
A: How about Korean food?
B: I think it's okay, but I like Indian better.

| Chinese | all right |
| French | delicious |

A: May I help you?
B: Yes. I'd like to know what today's special is.
A: Today's special is fish or chicken.
B: Well, I'll have fish, please.
A: And would you like anything to drink?
B: I'd like a glass of water, please.
A: Okay. Is that everything?
B: Yes.

| fish or pasta | wine |
| vegetarian or fish | orange juice |

Expressing Likes and Dislikes

Look at the phrases for expressing likes and dislikes. Listen and repeat.

Questions	Do you like vegetables? Is there any food that you dislike?
	What kind of food do you like? What are your favorite dishes?
	What do you think of Thai food? Do you prefer Thai or Indian food?
	Which do you like better, Chinese or Japanese food?
Expressing Likes	I kind of like Greek food. I like sweets. I really like Indian curries.
	I like salads a lot. I love chicken. I think Italian food is okay.
	I think barbequed food is good. I think noodles are great.
	I think Russian food is delicious. I think French cuisine is fantastic.
Expressing Dislikes	I don't like oily food. I dislike fried food. I can't stand raw fish.
	I hate spicy food. I don't think fast food is very good.
	I think omelets are not delicious at all. I think pickles are terrible.
Expressing Preferences	I prefer Korean food to Mexican. I like Indian food better than Thai.

 **Listen to the conversations and circle the food that both speakers like.**

1. Italian food / Indian food / Chinese food   **2.** sushi / tofu / chocolate   **3.** chicken / hamburger

Speak Out   **Fill in the blanks. Then, ask your partner the questions.**

1. Do you like _____?

2. Are there any _____ that you dislike?

3. What do you think of _____?

4. I can't stand _____. Are there any foods that you really dislike?

5. What is your favorite _____?

6. What do you think of _____?

7. Do you prefer _____ or _____?

8. Which do you like better, _____ or _____?

Speaking Strategy

Using Polite Expressions

When you are shopping, eating out, or talking to people in the workplace, you need to use polite expressions. Listen and repeat.

- I'd like to have a menu, please.
- I'd like to order, please.
- I'd like to know what today's special is.
- Could you tell me when the restaurant opens?
- Could you tell me how much the wine costs?
- Could you tell me where the washrooms are?

 **Speak Out 1** **Fill in the blanks. Then, read the sentences to your partner.**

I went to a restaurant yesterday. At first, I asked the waiter, "Excuse me. _____ you tell me what today's special is?" He said, "Today's special is _____." Then, I asked him, "_____ _____ to know how much today's special _____," and he said, "It costs 10,000 yen." Then, I asked him, "Could you tell me _____ the nearest bank is, please?"

 **Speak Out 2** **Change the sentences to be polite expressions. Then, read the sentences to your partner.**

1. I want an orange juice. → I'd like to have …, please.
2. I want to order French fries and a large Coca Cola. → I'd like to have …, please.
3. I want to have a menu. → I'd like to …, please.
4. I want to change my soup. → I'd like to …, please.
5. What's today's special? → I'd like to know …
6. What kind of dressing do you have? → I'd like to know …
7. What time does the restaurant close? → Could you tell me …, please?
8. How much is the juice? → Could you tell me …, please?
9. Where are the washrooms? → Could you tell me …, please?

Ordering in a Restaurant

Look at the questions and answers for ordering in a restaurant. Listen and repeat.

Questions   May I help you?   Can I help you?   Will that be spaghetti, fish or pizza?
Would you like spaghetti, fish or pizza?   Would you like soup or salad with that?
What would you like to drink?   Is that everything?   Is there anything else?
Could you tell me what today's special is?   Could I have some French fries?
What kind of dressing do you have?   What kind do you have?

Answers   Today, we have spaghetti, fish or pizza.   I'll have the spaghetti, please.
I'd like to have the lunch special, please.   I'd like the French dressing, please.

 **Listen In**   Look at the menu and listen to the conversations. Circle the total amount for the orders.

1. $10.00 / $11.00 / $12.00 / $13.00 / $14.00 / $15.00
2. $10.00 / $11.00 / $12.00 / $13.00 / $14.00 / $15.00
3. $10.00 / $11.00 / $12.00 / $13.00 / $14.00 / $15.00
4. $10.00 / $11.00 / $12.00 / $13.00 / $14.00 / $15.00

MENU
Daily Lunch Specials ·········· **$10.00**
• Spaghetti with Meat Sauce
• Fried Fish
• Vegetarian Pizza
* Served with Soup or Salad * Drink: Juice / Milk / Coffee

Other Main Dishes

Tomato and Broccoli Spaghetti	$8.00
Hamburger	$6.50

Side Dishes

French Fries	Large $4.50 / Small $3.00
Onion Soup	$5.00
Tomato Soup	$4.00

Salad

Seafood Salad	$10.50
Ceasar Salad	$7.50
Chef's Salad	$5.00

* Dressing: French / Thousand Island / Oil & Vinegar

Drinks

Coffee	$2.00
Espresso	$2.50
Cola	$2.00

 **Speak Out**   Read the conversation. Then, practice ordering food and drinks.

A: May I help you?
B: Yes. I'd like to have the lunch special, please.
A: Will that be spaghetti, fish, or pizza?
B: I'd like the pizza, please.
A: All right. Would you like soup or salad?
B: I'll have the soup, please.
A: I see. And what would you like to drink?
B: I'll have juice, please.
A: Okay. Is that everything?
B: Yes.
A: I'll be right back with your order.
B: Thank you.

WRAP IT UP

Write your answers to the questions. Then, ask your partner the questions. Use phrases for expressing likes and dislikes when you answer.

Example   **A:** What did you eat last night?
B: I ate a beef bowl and miso soup. I love Japanese food. How about you?
A: I ate fried noodles. I like Chinese food.

Questions	Your answers	Your partner's answers
1. What did you eat last night?		
2. What do you usually have for breakfast?		
3. What kind of drinks do you usually drink?		
4. What kind of food did you use to eat when you were younger?		
5. Which restaurants do you usually go to?		
6. What are some of your favorite foods?		
7. Can you cook anything?		
8. Do you think you could live without eating meat?		
9. Is there any food that you can't eat?		
10. What do you think are the top three cuisines in the world?		

Word Bank

Check (✔) the words that you know. If there are any words that you don't know, look them up in your dictionary.

Useful Phrases

- [ ] I'm in a bit of a hurry.
- [ ] I'll be right back.
- [ ] I'd appreciate that.
- [ ] Me, too.
- [ ] That's all.
- [ ] I can't stand …
- [ ] At first, …
- [ ] as soon as I can
- [ ] the best in the world
- [ ] not at all

Nouns

- [ ] anything
- [ ] everything
- [ ] cuisine
- [ ] dish
- [ ] fast food
- [ ] menu
- [ ] today's special
- [ ] noodle
- [ ] pasta
- [ ] spaghetti
- [ ] pizza
- [ ] omelet
- [ ] hamburger
- [ ] curry
- [ ] beef bowl
- [ ] raw fish
- [ ] soup
- [ ] miso soup
- [ ] French fries
- [ ] Ceasar salad
- [ ] dressing
- [ ] oil and vinegar

- [ ] Thousand Island
- [ ] meat sauce
- [ ] meat
- [ ] chicken
- [ ] pork
- [ ] vegetable
- [ ] pickles
- [ ] drink
- [ ] juice
- [ ] Espresso
- [ ] bottled water
- [ ] wine
- [ ] sweets
- [ ] chocolate
- [ ] chocoholic
- [ ] sir
- [ ] ma'am
- [ ] chef
- [ ] waiter
- [ ] waitress
- [ ] workplace
- [ ] restaurant
- [ ] washroom
- [ ] restroom

Verbs

- [ ] practice
- [ ] open
- [ ] close
- [ ] eat out
- [ ] have *something* for breakfast
- [ ] order
- [ ] change
- [ ] serve
- [ ] live without *something*
- [ ] prefer

- [ ] hate

Adjectives

- [ ] Chinese
- [ ] French
- [ ] Greek
- [ ] Indian
- [ ] Italian
- [ ] Japanese
- [ ] Korean
- [ ] Mexican
- [ ] Russian
- [ ] Spanish
- [ ] Thai
- [ ] Vietnamese
- [ ] vegetarian
- [ ] delicious
- [ ] better
- [ ] spicy
- [ ] oily
- [ ] fried
- [ ] deep-fried
- [ ] barbequed
- [ ] steamed
- [ ] boiled
- [ ] grilled
- [ ] daily
- [ ] unusual
- [ ] favorite
- [ ] nearest
- [ ] polite
- [ ] impolite

Adverbs and Prepositions

- [ ] a lot

The Future

I'm going to be a bird in the future.

Hmm ... I think that's going to be very difficult.

Read the conversations with your partner. Then, make new conversations using the words in the boxes.

1
A: What will you do after you graduate?
B: I'm going to travel around Europe.
A: Great. Who will you travel with?
B: I hope to travel with my brother. How about you?
A: I'm going to work at a hotel.
B: When will you start?
A: In April. I'm looking forward to working, but I'll miss school.

| Southeast Asia |
| for an electronics company   May |

| South America |
| for a computer company   September |

2
A: Who do you think is going to win the game tonight?
B: I'm sure that the Eagles will win.
A: I don't think so. I think the Lions are going to win because they're the home team.
B: Anyway, it will definitely be a good game.
A: I'm looking forward to watching it.
B: Me, too.

| I disagree.   will   probably |

| I doubt it.   will probably   certainly |

Future Tense Questions and Answers

Look at the future tense questions and answers. Listen and repeat.

Are you going to study English tonight? → Yes, I am. / No, I'm not.

Will they work at part-time jobs during the holidays? → Yes, they will. / No, they won't.

Who is she shopping with tomorrow? → She's shopping with her sister.

What are you looking forward to doing in the future? → I'm looking forward to traveling abroad.

Where does he plan to go this weekend? → He plans to go to Kyoto and Nara.

When do you hope to get married? → I hope to get married before I'm 30.

What do you want to be in the future? → I want to be a teacher.

 **Listen to the conversations and read the statements. Circle T for true and F for false. Correct the false statements.**

1. James and Atsushi are going to have some Middle Eastern food for lunch.   T / F

2. The woman and her friends are going to watch some movies on the weekend.   T / F

3. The man is going to go to John's house for a barbeque.   T / F

4. Both of the speakers will travel during the New Year's holidays.   T / F

5. The speakers are going to get married to each other.   T / F

6. The man doesn't want to have children.   T / F

 **Fill in the blanks with the words in the box. Then, ask your partner the questions.**

| are   will   looking   who   what   where   when |

1. _____ are you going to do tonight?

2. _____ you travel anywhere during the holidays?

3. _____ are you going to meet after school today?

4. What time _____ you going to go home tonight?

5. What are you _____ forward to doing in the future?

6. _____ do you plan to start working?

7. _____ do you hope to live when you're older?

Agreeing and Disagreeing

When you respond to others' opinions, you can use phrases for agreeing and disagreeing. Listen and repeat.

A 69

Agreeing	• I agree. • I agree with you. • I think so, too. • I don't think so, either. • You're right. • Absolutely. • Definitely.
Disagreeing	• I disagree. • I don't think so. • I don't think you're right. • I doubt it. • I don't think that's possible.

 **Speak Out 1**   **Fill in the blanks. Then, read the conversations with your partner.**

1 **A:** I think the Giants are going to win the game tonight.

   B: _____ I think the Tigers will win.

2 **A:** I think home phones and public phones will disappear from our lives soon.

   B: _____ Everyone will have a smartphone.

3 **A:** I don't think people will live on the moon in the near future.

   B: _____ It will take more than one century.

4 **A:** I think that it'll rain tomorrow.

   B: _____ I think it'll be sunny.

 **Speak Out 2**   **Read the sentences to your partner. Use phrases for agreeing or disagreeing and make some comments when you respond.**

1. I think we're going to have snow here this winter.
2. I think eSports will become an Olympic sport soon.
3. I don't think we will run out of oil in the future.
4. I think the population of Japan will increase next year.
5. I think the cost of food will decrease in the future.
6. I don't think whales will become extinct in the future.
7. I think manga will become more popular around the world.
8. I think all cars will have solar batteries in a decade or so.

Expressing Certainty and Uncertainty

Look at the phrases for expressing certainty and uncertainty. Listen and repeat.

Expressing Certainty	I think she'll definitely get a job as a model.
	I'm definitely going to buy a car. I definitely won't be a politician.
	I'm certain it will rain tonight. I'm sure that I'll go abroad next year.
	I'm sure that he's not going to pass the exam.
Expressing Uncertainty	I think he'll probably work for a travel agency.
	I'm probably going to buy a bike. I probably won't go out tomorrow.
	I think she's probably not going to be a lawyer.
	I think it may snow tonight. I might travel around Europe soon.
	I'm not sure if I can get a ticket for the concert.

 Listen to the conversations between Mike and Sally. Circle the correct words and complete the sentences.

1. Tonight, [Mike / Sally] probably won't finish the homework and Sally will [definitely / probably] cook at home.

2. Mike is [sure that he's / probably] going jogging tomorrow morning and Sally [will definitely / might] join him.

3. Mike will [definitely / probably] take the flower arrangement class. As for the tonight's TV documentary, he [is definitely going to / might] watch it.

 Ask your partner the questions. Use phrases for expressing certainty and uncertainty when you answer.

1. Do you think it's going to rain tomorrow?
2. Do you think trains are going to be faster in the future?
3. Do you think people will travel to Mars someday?
4. Are you going to cook at home tonight?
5. Do you think you'll get married before you're 30?
6. What's your plan for next week?
7. What are you going to do after you graduate from this school?

WRAP IT UP

Talk about the future with your partner. Use phrases for expressing certainty and uncertainty when you give your opinions.

Example
A: What do you think restaurants will be like in the future?
B: I think there will definitely be more fast food restaurants.
A: I agree.

Example
A: What will the weather be like tomorrow?
B: I'm sure that it'll be sunny.
A: I don't think so. I think it'll probably rain.

Example
A: Do you think Japan is going to have more robots in the future?
B: I definitely think so.
A: Me, too. I think there will definitely be robots working in restaurants and hotels.

Example
A: What are you doing during the holidays?
B: I'm not sure, but I'm probably going back to my hometown.
A: I see. Well, I might travel somewhere.

restaurants	hotels	food	sports
the Olympics	the Hanshin Tigers	English	Japan
robots	people	parents	children
homes	this school	work	computers
TV	music	fashion	pets
cars	trains	travel	politics
the world	the moon	the environment	nature
weather	tonight	next weekend	holidays

Word Bank

Check (✔) the words that you know. If there are any words that you don't know, look them up in your dictionary.

Useful Phrases

- [ ] It depends on how I feel.
- [ ] I've heard it's very good.
- [ ] As for …
- [ ] after I graduate
- [ ] before I'm 30
- [ ] when I'm older
- [ ] in the future
- [ ] during the holidays
- [ ] at midnight
- [ ] for lunch

Nouns

- [ ] the sun
- [ ] the moon
- [ ] Mars
- [ ] century
- [ ] decade
- [ ] opinion
- [ ] certainty
- [ ] uncertainty
- [ ] documentary
- [ ] Southeast Asia
- [ ] South America
- [ ] fast food restaurant
- [ ] electronics company
- [ ] solar battery
- [ ] public phone
- [ ] home phone
- [ ] smartphone
- [ ] oil
- [ ] cost
- [ ] environment
- [ ] weather
- [ ] nature

- [ ] population
- [ ] politics
- [ ] whale
- [ ] kid
- [ ] politician
- [ ] lawyer
- [ ] top model
- [ ] flower arrangement
- [ ] barbeque
- [ ] Olympic sport
- [ ] home team
- [ ] close game

Verbs

- [ ] be sunny
- [ ] rain
- [ ] snow
- [ ] increase
- [ ] decrease
- [ ] be out of money
- [ ] run out of *something*
- [ ] become extinct
- [ ] become popular
- [ ] get married to *someone*
- [ ] have children
- [ ] own a house
- [ ] host
- [ ] come along
- [ ] join
- [ ] take a class
- [ ] fall asleep
- [ ] pass an exam
- [ ] go jogging
- [ ] have a plan
- [ ] plan to start *something*
- [ ] plan to visit *a place*

- [ ] plan to go to *a place*
- [ ] hope to have *something*
- [ ] hope to live in *a place*
- [ ] hope to be *something*
- [ ] work at a hotel
- [ ] work for a travel agency
- [ ] travel with *someone*
- [ ] travel around *a place*
- [ ] win a game
- [ ] lose a game
- [ ] get a ticket
- [ ] hand in *something*
- [ ] rent
- [ ] borrow
- [ ] agree
- [ ] disagree
- [ ] doubt

Adjectives

- [ ] certain
- [ ] sure
- [ ] Middle Eastern
- [ ] traditional
- [ ] modern
- [ ] possible

Adverbs and Prepositions

- [ ] definitely
- [ ] absolutely
- [ ] certainly
- [ ] probably
- [ ] someday
- [ ] yet
- [ ] either

Speak Out 1 **Fill in the blanks with the words in the boxes. Use capitalization when necessary. Then, read the conversations with your partner.**

1

A: Hi. You look tired. What's up?

B: Well, I _____ a very busy weekend. _____ Saturday, I practiced basketball all day and then on Sunday, I swam _____ about three hours.

A: Wow! That's tiring.

B: Yup. So, _____ are you going to do tonight?

A: Yuichi and I are _____ go out and eat some Middle Eastern food.

B: Can I come along?

A: _____.

B: _____ shall we meet?

A: _____ meet at 5:15 in front of the school.

B: Okay.

> what   sure   on   had   let's   going to   where   for

2

A: What _____ of food do you like?

B: I _____ Japanese food.

A: Well, I _____ Japanese food is okay, but I prefer Thai food.

B: Wow! Thai food is _____ spicy.

A: I _____ spicy food. How about you?

B: I _____ spicy food. I don't think it's delicious _____.

A: So, where do you want to eat then?

B: Let's eat Italian. I know a great restaurant.

A: I think Italian food is _____. That's a good choice.

> think   kind   can't stand   love   so   prefer   at all   fantastic

3

A: _____ I help you?

B: Yes. I'd _____ have the lunch special, please.

A: All right. _____ that be spaghetti, fish or pizza?

B: _____ the pizza, please.

A: _____ you like soup or salad?

B: I'd like a salad with oil and vinegar dressing, _____.

A: Okay. And _____ would you like to drink?

B: I'll have a coffee.

A: Is that _____, sir?

B: Yes.

A: I'll _____ right back, sir.

B: Thank you.

| be   please   may   like to   what   will   would   I'll have   everything |

🔊 *Speak Out 2*   **Talk about one of the topics. Keep the talk going for at least 1 minute.**

| this morning | | last weekend | | food you love | | eating out |

| weekend activities | | your favorite restaurant |

| your plan for next weekend | | your plan for the next holiday |

🔊 *Speak Out 3*   **Plan with your partner what you want to do together this Friday, Saturday, and Sunday. Also, decide where and when you will meet.**

Friday	Saturday	Sunday

 *Speak Out 4* **Make a short presentation about one of the topics. Refer to the format and example phrases in the box when you prepare.**

- Last weekend   • Your favorite restaurant
- The top two cuisines in the world   • Your plan for next year
- The future of one of the following: hotels, sports, Japan, fashion, TV, or the world

Introduction	Hello everyone. Today, I'm going to talk about what I did last weekend.
General Feeling / Main Idea	I had a very difficult weekend. I'll tell you why.
Details	First, on Friday night, I … Second, on Saturday, I … On Sunday, I had many troubles.
Conclusion	So, as you can see, my weekend had many troubles and made me very tired.
Summary	It was a very difficult weekend but I learned a lot about getting up on time.

 *Speak Out 5* **Ask your partner the questions. Always answer with at least two sentences and continue the conversation with follow-up questions.**

1. How was your weekend?
2. What did you do yesterday?
3. What did you do this morning?
4. What did you do during the last school holiday?
5. Do you feel like going hiking tomorrow?
6. Are you a good cook?
7. What do you usually have for breakfast?
8. What kind of food do you like?
9. Are there any dishes that you can't stand?
10. What do you plan to do this weekend?
11. What will you do after you graduate?
12. Where do you hope to live when you're older?
13. Do you think people will live on the moon someday?
14. Do you think people will still need driver's licenses in the future?
15. Do you think AI will take care of older people in the future?

Listen In 1   Listen to the conversations and answer the questions.

A
74-79

1. **a)** When did Pete go out with his family? _____

   b) Name three things that Pete did with his family. _____

2. **a)** What does the man have tickets for? When is it? _____

   b) Where and what time will the two people meet? _____

3. **a)** What does the woman hate? _____

   b) Where and what will the two people eat tonight? _____

4. **a)** What does the woman order? _____

   b) What kind of coffee does the woman order? _____

5. **a)** How many people are going to the game center? _____

   b) Where is the game center? _____

6. **a)** What does the man want to do and when? _____

   b) Will the woman join him? _____

Listen In 2   Listen to the conversations and read the statements.
Circle T for true and F for false. Correct the false statements.

A
80-85

1. **a)** The speakers will go see a movie on Saturday.   T / F

   b) They will meet at 2 o'clock on Sunday.   T / F

2. **a)** On the 18th, the man met some friends for dinner.   T / F

   b) The speakers will go sing karaoke tonight.   T / F

3. **a)** The woman likes sushi.   T / F

   b) The man likes to eat chocolate every day.   T / F

4. **a)** The woman orders spaghetti, soup and salad.   T / F

   b) The woman orders something to drink.   T / F

5. **a)** The man is going to celebrate his 25th birthday with family in Hokkaido.   T / F

   b) The man hopes to own his own house in the future.   T / F

6. **a)** The man is going to take the tea ceremony class.   T / F

   b) The man will watch the documentary about the history of Okinawa.   T / F

Travel

Read the conversations with your partner. Then, make new conversations using the words in the boxes.

 1

A: Excuse me. Is there a bank near here?

B: There sure is. It's down this street on the left. It's across the street from the bookstore.

A: Okay. Down this street on the left?

B: Yeah. It's a red building.

A: I see. Thank you very much.

B: You're welcome. Have a good day.

just past	I appreciate your help.
next to	Thank you so much.

 2

A: Excuse me. Could you tell me how to get to the Science Museum?

B: Sure. Walk down this street until you come to the first light and turn left.

A: So, walk down this street and turn left at the first light?

B: That's right. It's on the other side of the park.

A: I think I got it. Thank you for your help.

B: No problem.

get to	next to
see	in front of

Talking about Location

Look at the phrases for talking about location. Listen and repeat. B/02

Asking for Location	Could you tell me where the Japanese Embassy is, please?
	Do you know where the parking lot is? Is there a drugstore near here?
Describing Location	It's down this street on the right. It's just past the convenience store.
	It's on the corner of Main Avenue and 3rd Street. It's around the corner.
	It's across the street from the library. It's on the other side of the park.
	It's next to the travel agency. It's between the bakery and the museum.
	It's opposite the bookstore. It's behind the mall. It's right there.
Ending Conversations	Thank you so much. Thank you for your help. I appreciate your help.
	You're welcome. Anytime. No problem. Have a good day.

Listen In — **Listen to the conversations and match the places with the letters on the map.** B/03-08

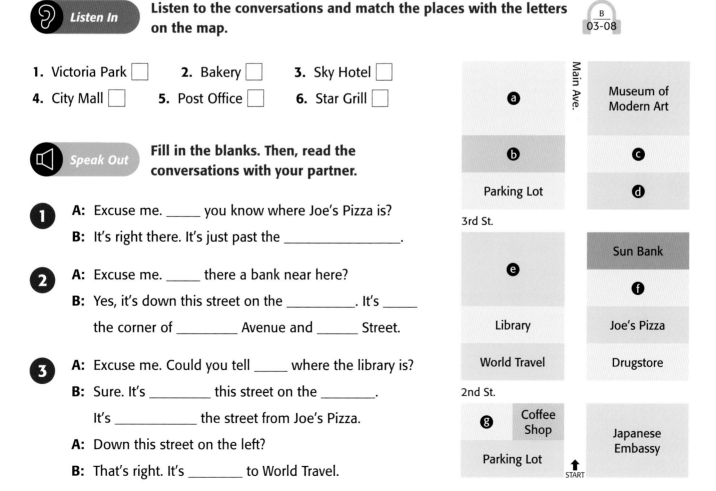

1. Victoria Park ☐   2. Bakery ☐   3. Sky Hotel ☐
4. City Mall ☐   5. Post Office ☐   6. Star Grill ☐

Speak Out — **Fill in the blanks. Then, read the conversations with your partner.**

1
A: Excuse me. _____ you know where Joe's Pizza is?
B: It's right there. It's just past the _____.

2
A: Excuse me. _____ there a bank near here?
B: Yes, it's down this street on the _____. It's _____
the corner of _____ Avenue and _____ Street.

3
A: Excuse me. Could you tell _____ where the library is?
B: Sure. It's _____ this street on the _____.
It's _____ the street from Joe's Pizza.
A: Down this street on the left?
B: That's right. It's _____ to World Travel.

Map labels: Main Ave., Museum of Modern Art, a, b, c, d, Parking Lot, 3rd St., e, Sun Bank, f, Library, Joe's Pizza, World Travel, Drugstore, 2nd St., g, Coffee Shop, Parking Lot, Japanese Embassy, START

Speaking Strategy

Asking Comparison Questions

Asking questions that make comparisons about places and things can make conversations more personal and interesting. Listen and repeat.

> What is more interesting to you, traveling alone or traveling in a group?
> What is the most interesting place that you've traveled to?
> What is your least favorite way to travel?
> Which would you prefer, going shopping or going to a museum in a foreign country?
> What is the best place to visit in Japan?
> What is the worst trip you've had?

 **Speak Out 1** Fill in the blanks with the correct words. Then, read the conversations with your partner.

1
A: What is your _____ way to travel?
B: Oh, definitely by plane. I love flying.

2
A: Which would you _____, camping by the beach or staying in a hotel?
B: I prefer camping by the beach. I think it's more beautiful.

3
A: What is the _____ travel experience you've ever had?
B: Oh, that was in high school in Kyoto. I was sick for three days.

 **Speak Out 2** Ask your partner the questions.

1. What is the best trip you've had?
2. What is your favorite Japanese city? Why?
3. Where would you like to travel next?
4. What's the best place to visit in Japan?
5. What's the worst travel experience you've ever had?
6. Which would you prefer, to travel in Brazil or in Egypt?
7. What is your least favorite way to travel?
8. Which is more interesting to you, going hiking or going swimming in the ocean?
9. Where have you traveled in Japan? Which place was most beautiful?
10. Where have you traveled abroad? What places were most interesting?

Asking for and Giving Directions

Look at the phrases for asking for and giving directions. Listen and repeat.

Asking for Directions	Could you tell me how to get to the Union Botanical Garden, please?
	How can I get to the Pacific Aquarium from here?
Giving Directions	Walk down this street. Go straight until you come to the first light.
	Keep walking until the very end. Walk for about two minutes.
	Walk past the National Art Gallery. Turn left at the next street.
	Turn right at the second corner. Go through the park.
	Cross 6th Street. You'll see it on your left.

 **Listen In**   Listen to the conversations and match the places with the letters on the map.

1. National Art Gallery ☐
2. Seaside Café ☐
3. Traveler's Center ☐
4. Pacific Aquarium ☐
5. Fisherman's Market ☐
6. Grand Hotel ☐
7. Union Botanical Garden ☐
8. Dolphins ☐

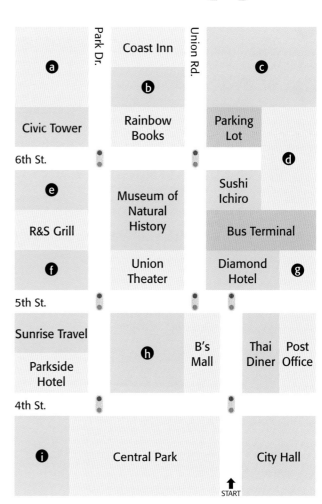

Speak Out   Ask your partner the questions.

1. How can I get to the post office from here?
2. Could you tell me how to get to the Parkside Hotel, please?
3. Do you know where the Union Theater is?
4. How can I get to the bus terminal from here?
5. Is there a travel agency near here?
6. Could you tell me where the R&S Grill is, please?
7. Do you know where the Coast Inn is?
8. How can I get to the Civic Tower from here?
9. Is there a sushi restaurant near here?
10. Could you tell me how to get to the Museum of Natural History, please?

WRAP IT UP

Imagine you are a traveler. Decide where you want to go and ask your partner questions. Use phrases for talking about location and asking for and giving directions.

Example

A: Excuse me. Could you tell me how to get to the Rose Music Center, please?

B: Sure. Walk down this street and turn right at the first corner. Then, go straight for about five minutes. It's on the corner of 7th Street and Rose Avenue.

A: So, turn right at the first corner and go straight. It's on the corner of 7th Street and Rose Avenue?

B: That's right. It's the blue building.

A: Thank you so much.

B: You're welcome.

Example

A: Excuse me. Is there a library near here?

B: There sure is. Go straight until you come to the very end and turn left. Then, turn right at the first light. It's just past the Clock Tower.

A: Let me repeat that. Go straight until the very end and turn left. Then, turn right at the first light. It's next to the Clock Tower?

B: That's correct. You'll see it on your left.

A: Okay. I think I got it. I appreciate your help.

B: No problem. Have a good day.

A: You, too.

Metro Zoo		Green Dr.	Parking Lot	Pine Ave.	Japanese Embassy	Oakwood Restaurant	Spring Hotel	Spring Rd.	Tasty Grill	Rose Ave.	Asian Kitchen	
												Hilltop Mall

9th St.

Museum of African Art	Golden Hotel	City Library		Wonderful Gifts	Traveler's Center	Sky Bank		Bistro Paris		Sunny Theater	
	Moon Theater			Pine Aquarium				Mike's Pizza		Bus Terminal	
						Farmer's Market					
Fantastic Café	Green Bakery	Clock Tower		Star Amusement Park				Sushi Sakura		Tom's Books	
											Eastend Market Place

8th St.

| National Botanical Garden | | City Hall | | Angel Drugstore | Century Travel | Post Office | | Police Station | | Rose Music Center | |
| | | | | Parkfront Records | Parking Lot | | | Best Inn | | | Napoli Diner |

7th St.

| Universal Travel | Parkside Hotel | Memorial Park | | Water Tower | Fine Bank | | Max Jewelry | | Café 7 | R-Mart |

START

Word Bank

Check (✔) the words that you know. If there are any words that you don't know, look them up in your dictionary.

Useful Phrases

- [ ] Excuse me.
- [ ] There sure is.
- [ ] Let's see.
- [ ] Let me see.
- [ ] Let me repeat that.
- [ ] That's correct.
- [ ] That's right.
- [ ] Right.
- [ ] Yup.
- [ ] I see.
- [ ] I think I got it.
- [ ] Thanks a lot.
- [ ] You're welcome.
- [ ] My pleasure.
- [ ] No problem.
- [ ] Anytime.
- [ ] You, too.
- [ ] The easiest way is …
- [ ] It's called …
- [ ] on the left
- [ ] on your right
- [ ] across the street from …
- [ ] on the other side of …
- [ ] on the corner of … and …
- [ ] around the corner
- [ ] at the very end of the street
- [ ] more interesting
- [ ] the most interesting
- [ ] the best
- [ ] the worst

Nouns

- [ ] map
- [ ] tower
- [ ] light
- [ ] avenue
- [ ] road
- [ ] drive
- [ ] embassy
- [ ] city hall
- [ ] police station
- [ ] post office
- [ ] bank
- [ ] bus terminal
- [ ] parking lot
- [ ] park
- [ ] aquarium
- [ ] botanical garden
- [ ] museum
- [ ] gallery
- [ ] music center
- [ ] theater
- [ ] bookstore
- [ ] drugstore
- [ ] jewelry store
- [ ] travel agency
- [ ] traveler's center
- [ ] hotel
- [ ] inn
- [ ] mall
- [ ] market
- [ ] mart
- [ ] bakery
- [ ] coffee shop
- [ ] café
- [ ] kitchen
- [ ] diner
- [ ] bistro
- [ ] grill
- [ ] steak restaurant
- [ ] seafood
- [ ] ocean
- [ ] iceberg
- [ ] science
- [ ] natural history

Verbs

- [ ] give directions
- [ ] walk down
- [ ] go straight
- [ ] go through
- [ ] keep walking
- [ ] turn
- [ ] cross
- [ ] come to *a place*
- [ ] get to *a place*
- [ ] go out *a place*
- [ ] have a great time
- [ ] decide

Adjectives

- [ ] favorite
- [ ] complicated
- [ ] tasty

Adverbs and Prepositions

- [ ] next to
- [ ] between
- [ ] opposite
- [ ] in front of
- [ ] behind
- [ ] past
- [ ] right there
- [ ] politely

Entertainment

Read the conversations with your partner. Then, make new conversations using the words in the boxes.

1

A: Island Cinema. Can I help you?

B: Yes. I'd like to know what time *Spiderman* is playing in the evening, please?

A: Sure. It starts at 7:15 and 9:20.

B: I see. Is there an afternoon show tomorrow?

A: Yes, there is. It starts at 1:00.

B: Sorry, but could you say that again, please?

A: Sure. It starts at 1:00.

B: Okay. Thank you very much.

A: You're welcome. Have a good day.

7:45 and 9:30   a late show tonight repeat that
7:30 and 9:45   an early show tomorrow say that one more time

2

A: What kind of music do you like?

B: I love rock music.

A: What was the last album that you bought?

B: It was Queen.

A: So, what do you think of it?

B: I think it's really good.

A: Would you recommend it?

B: Oh, yeah. I definitely think you should listen to Queen. Their sound is so powerful and I love the singer's voice.

What's your favorite kind of music? I really like it.   If you have time,
What music do you like best? I think it's great.   I think that

Asking for and Giving Information

Look at the phrases for asking for and giving information. Listen and repeat.

Asking for Information	Could you tell me your opening hours, please?
	I'd like to know your opening and closing times, please.
	Could you tell me what time *Star Wars 15* is playing in the evening?
	Is there a late show tonight?
	I'd like to know how much the tickets cost, please.
Giving Information	We open at 10:00 in the morning and close at 9:00 at night.
	We're open from 9:30 a.m. until 8:30 p.m. We're closed on Mondays.
	The store is closed every Tuesday. The movie starts at 6:00 and 8:15.
	The tickets cost five dollars for children under the age of 12.

Listen In   **Listen to the telephone conversations and complete the sentences.** B 20-23

1. The movie starts at _____ and _____ in the evening, and the late show starts at _____ o'clock.

2. The animal park is _____ from 10:00 a.m. until _____ p.m., and it is closed on _____.
   The tickets cost _____ dollars for adults and children, and 10 dollars for seniors _____ the age of 60.

3. The store opens at 10:30 _____ morning and closes at _____ at night.

4. The tickets cost _____ dollars for adults, _____ dollars for children under the age of _____, and free for
   children _____ the age of five.

Speak Out   **Make questions about Downtown Theater. Then, ask your partner the questions.**
Use phrases for giving information when you answer.

1. Could you tell me _____
   _____?

2. I'd like to know _____
   _____.

3. Is there _____?

4. _____

5. _____

> **Downtown Theater**
> Open from 12:30 p.m. until 4:00 a.m.
> Closed on Wednesdays
>
> *Star Wars*
> Afternoon Show ▸ 1:15 and 3:45
> Evening Show ▸ 5:10 and 9:20
> Late Show ▸ 1:00
> Adults: $12 (Seniors over 60: $10)
> Children under 12: $8 (Under 4: Free)

Speaking Strategy

Asking for Repetition

When you want to be sure about the information you hear, you can use phrases for asking for repetition. Listen and repeat.

> • Could you say that again, please? • Could you repeat that, please?   • When was that again?
> • I'm sorry, but did you say 10 o'clock?   • Sorry, but how much was that again?   • Sorry?

 **Fill in the blanks. Then, read the conversations with your partner.**

1 **A:** I'd like to know what time *Vampire* is playing tonight, please.

 B: Sure. It starts at 6:15 and 8:45.

 A: _____

 B: It starts at 6:15 and 8:45.

 A: Thank you.

2 **A:** Could you tell me your opening and closing times, please?

 B: Sure, we open at 9:30 in the morning and close at 10:00 at night.

 A: _____

 B: We're open from 9:30 a.m. until 10:00 p.m. And the tickets costs 25 Euros.

 A: _____

 B: Twenty-five Euros.

 A: I see. Thanks.

Speak Out 2 **Fill in the blanks. Then, tell your partner the information. Use phrases for asking for repetition when you hear the information.**

1. The movie starts at _____ and _____ in the afternoon.

2. We're open from _____ a.m. until _____ p.m.

3. It costs ____ Euros to enter the amusement park.

4. The park is closed every _____.

5. The tickets cost ____ pounds for adults and ____ pounds for seniors over the age of 60.

Talking about Entertainment

Look at the phrases for talking about entertainment. Listen and repeat.

Questions	Do you like watching TV? Did you see the new *Batman* movie?
	Have you ever played video games? What kind of books do you like?
	What's your favorite kind of music? What was the last movie that you saw?
	How's the new comic book that you're reading? What do you think of it?
	How was the movie that you saw? Would you recommend it?
Recommendations	I definitely think you should read it. If you have time, you should see it.
	If you have the money, you should buy that game.
	I recommend that you go there because the rides are cheap.
	You shouldn't see that show because the acting is not very good.
	I don't recommend it because the story is not interesting.

 **Listen to the conversations and read the statements. Circle T for true and F for false. Correct the false statements.**

1. The man recommends that the woman see the movie because it is funny.   T / F
2. The woman doesn't recommend the new book because the story is too complicated.   T / F
3. The man likes the amusement park because the rides are cheap.   T / F
4. The woman thinks the man should read other horror comics.   T / F
5. The man doesn't recommend the video game because the story is not interesting.   T / F

 **Fill in the blanks. Then, ask your partner the questions. Use phrases for recommendations when you answer.**

1. Do you like _____?
2. What was the last _____ that you _____?
3. What kind of _____ do you like?
4. What _____ would you recommend?
5. What's your favorite kind of _____?
6. Have you ever _____?
7. Did you _____?

WRAP IT UP

Talk about entertainment with your partner. Ask as many questions as you can and keep the conversations going.

Example
A: What kind of movies do you like?
B: I love action movies.
A: Me, too. What was the last movie that you saw?
B: I saw the new Disney movie last week.
A: What do you think of it?
B: It was great because the special effects are so cool. I definitely think you should see it.

Example
A: Do you like watching TV?
B: Not very much. How about you?
A: I like watching TV a lot.
B: What kind of TV programs do you like?
A: I love sports. I recommend that you watch pro wrestling because it's so exciting.

Example
A: Do you play video games very often?
B: Of course. I play them almost every day.
A: Wow. What's your favorite kind of game?
B: I like Tetris. Last night I played it for about three hours. It's a great game. Have you ever played?

movies	adventure	jazz	sports
books	comedy	hip hop	video games
comic books	romance	gospel	role-playing games
games on a phone	mystery	TV programs	card games
horror	music	game shows	eSports
science fiction	pop	dramas	puzzle games
fantasy	rock	talk shows	racing games
action	classical	animation	fighting games

Word Bank

Check (✔) the words that you know. If there are any words that you don't know, look them up in your dictionary.

Useful Phrases

- [ ] Can I help you?
- [ ] Jim speaking.
- [ ] Got it.
- [ ] That sounds fun.
- [ ] I like many kinds.
- [ ] I like it a lot.
- [ ] Not very much.
- [ ] It's free for …
- [ ] the last movie that you saw
- [ ] as many … as you can
- [ ] the other day
- [ ] under the age of 12
- [ ] over the age of 60
- [ ] on the computer

Nouns

- [ ] entertainment
- [ ] animal park
- [ ] information
- [ ] opening hours
- [ ] opening time
- [ ] closing time
- [ ] afternoon show
- [ ] evening show
- [ ] late show
- [ ] ride
- [ ] ticket
- [ ] Euro
- [ ] adult
- [ ] senior
- [ ] music
- [ ] sound
- [ ] pop
- [ ] rock

- [ ] jazz
- [ ] hip hop
- [ ] gospel
- [ ] singer
- [ ] voice
- [ ] TV program
- [ ] game show
- [ ] talk show
- [ ] sports
- [ ] pro wrestling
- [ ] film
- [ ] story
- [ ] special effects
- [ ] acting
- [ ] action movie
- [ ] animation
- [ ] drama
- [ ] suspense
- [ ] thriller
- [ ] musical
- [ ] science fiction
- [ ] fantasy
- [ ] adventure
- [ ] comedy
- [ ] romance
- [ ] mystery
- [ ] novel
- [ ] comic book
- [ ] video game
- [ ] role-playing game
- [ ] card game
- [ ] board game
- [ ] racing game
- [ ] fighting game
- [ ] puzzle game
- [ ] repetition
- [ ] recommendation

- [ ] living dead
- [ ] zombie

Verbs

- [ ] be sure about *something*
- [ ] play
- [ ] watch
- [ ] enter
- [ ] start
- [ ] turn up the volume
- [ ] keep *something* going
- [ ] recommend

Adjectives

- [ ] classical
- [ ] powerful
- [ ] funny
- [ ] cool
- [ ] scary
- [ ] horror
- [ ] other
- [ ] earlier

Adverbs and Prepositions

- [ ] ever
- [ ] almost
- [ ] a little bit
- [ ] though

Staying Healthy

What's your morning routine?

First, I find a shellfish. Then, I open it. Finally, I eat it.

Read the conversations with your partner. Then, make new conversations using the words in the boxes.

1
A: What's your morning routine?
B: Well, I usually wake up around 6:30. First, I drink a glass of water. After that, I do 50 push-ups and 50 sit-ups.
A: That's great!
B: Next, I go for a walk for about half an hour, and then I take a shower. Finally, I have breakfast.
A: It sounds healthy.

jog for about 40 minutes tiring
do weight training for about 20 minutes difficult

2
A: What are you drinking?
B: It's a power drink that I have every morning.
A: How do you make it?
B: First, you need two cups of soy milk, a frozen banana, some peanut butter, and a few ice cubes. Next, put all the ingredients into a blender and mix. Finally, pour the juice into a glass and enjoy.
A: That seems extremely easy.

every night After that very
every day Then really

Describing Routines

Look at the phrases for describing routines. Listen and repeat.

- First, I get up around 7 a.m. and do some stretching. • After that, I run for about 20 minutes.
- Next, I swim for about 15 minutes, and then do some weight training for about an hour.
- Then, I do some more stretching until I cool down. • Finally, I take a sauna and a shower.

Listen In **Listen to the conversations and put the events in the correct order.** B 32-34

1. ☐ get up at 6 a.m. ☐ work out in the gym ☐ go for a run ☐ check e-mail ☐ have breakfast
2. ☐ play a few games ☐ finish around 7 p.m. ☐ practice shots ☐ do stretching exercises
   ☐ clean the courts ☐ hit the balls around
3. ☐ take a shower ☐ have classes ☐ walk the dog ☐ wake up around 10 a.m. ☐ have lunch
   ☐ study or work part-time ☐ ride bicycle to school

Speak Out 1 **Look at the daily routine of Takako, a long-distance runner, and describe it to your partner.**

In the morning
1. get up at 5:30
2. eat a light breakfast
3. run 15 km and then do stretching exercises
4. take a shower
5. meet with her manager

In the afternoon and evening
1. have lunch
2. work out at a gym and then take a shower
3. cook dinner
4. watch TV
5. go to bed around 10:00

Speak Out 2 **Fill in the blanks and complete your morning routine. Then, tell your partner about it.**

First, _____.

After that, _____.

Next, _____.

Then, _____.

Finally, _____.

Using Numbers

If you get accustomed to reading numbers, you will be able to use number expressions easily in conversations. Listen and repeat.

> - I usually wake up at ten to six and start jogging at five past seven.   - He weighs 100 kilograms.
> - The average body temperature is 35.5°C.   - I spent $204.49 on medicine last year.
> - The yoga mattress that I bought was ¥2,550.   - I take in about 1,800 kilocalories per day.
> - He paid ¥13,000 to his sports club.   - She ran 50 kilometers and collected ¥1,567,840 for charity.
> - The world population in 2020 was more than 7.8 billion.
> - In a full marathon, athletes are supposed to run 26 miles or 42.195 kilometers.
> - I took a nap for half an hour in the afternoon.   - I drink 1/3 of a cup of vinegar for my health.

 **Speak Out 1**   **Match the numbers on the left with the correct expressions on the right. Then, read the sentences to your partner.**

1. Tom usually wakes up at **5:50**.
2. Linda paid **$1,240** to her sports club last year.
3. He needs to take in **2,200 kcal** per day.
4. I left home for jogging at **7:15**.
5. My temperature was about **37.8°C** last night.
6. I work out for **2.5 hours** every weekend.
7. My family spent **¥1,650,000** on groceries last year.
8. Bob bought a suit and it was **$99.99**.
9. I used **1/4** of a package of tofu for the miso soup.

- one thousand two hundred forty dollars
- thirty-seven point eight degrees Celsius
- ten to six
- quarter past seven
- one quarter
- two thousand two hundred kilocalories
- ninety-nine dollars and ninety-nine cents
- two and a half hours
- one million, six hundred and fifty thousand yen

 **Speak Out 2**   **Ask your partner the questions.**

1. What time did you get up and leave home this morning?
2. How much does it cost to join a sports club?
3. Do you know what the temperature is today?
4. How much water did you drink yesterday?
5. How many kilometers do you think you could walk right now?
6. Do you know the population of Japan, Tokyo, Osaka, or your hometown?
7. How long do you usually sleep on weekdays and on the weekends?

Giving Instructions

Look at the phrases for giving instructions. Listen and repeat.

> - Now, I'm going to tell you how to make a healthy sandwich.
> - First, prepare two slices of bread, a tomato, some lettuce, celery, cheese, and butter.
> - Next, cut the tomato, celery, and cheese into thin slices.
> - Then, toast two slices of bread. When they're finished, put some butter on them.
> - After that, put some lettuce, the sliced tomato, celery, and cheese on one slice of bread.
> - Finally, put the other slice of bread on top and enjoy the sandwich.

 **Listen to the recipes for healthy drinks and put the sentences in the correct order.**

1. ☐ Put all the ingredients into a blender and mix.   ☐ Enjoy the Blueberry Tofu Wonder.
   ☐ Cut up the banana.   ☐ Prepare the ingredients.   ☐ Pour the juice into a glass.
2. ☐ Put the bananas into a blender.   ☐ Turn on the blender and mix.   ☐ Slice up the other banana.
   ☐ Cut up one banana.   ☐ Put the banana into the freezer.   ☐ Prepare the ingredients.
   ☐ Add ice cubes, yogurt, and water.   ☐ Take out the frozen banana after an hour.

 **Fill in the blanks and complete the recipe. Then, tell your partner how to make Cucumber Salad.**

Cucumber Salad
- 1/2 cup of plain yogurt
- 1 tablespoon of oil
- 1/3 teaspoon of salt
- 1 1/2 teaspoons of lemon juice
- 2 cucumbers
- 1 tomato
- some celery
- some lettuce

1. Cut up the celery into small pieces and put them into a bowl.
2. Add yogurt, _____, lemon _____, salt, and mix.
3. Cut the cucumbers and tomato into thin slices.
4. Put the sliced _____ into the bowl, and mix.
5. Put some _____ and the sliced tomatoes on a plate.
6. Put the mixture on top.

WRAP IT UP

Write your answers to the questions. Then, ask your partner the questions. Express your opinions when you answer.

Example
A: What do you do to stay healthy?
B: Well, first I jog for about two kilometers every morning and then I drink a glass of fresh juice. And … I also try to sleep for seven hours at least every day.
A: Wow. You're very careful about your health, aren't you?

Questions	Your answers
1. What do you do to stay healthy?	
2. Are you careful about what you eat?	
3. How many hours of sleep do you usually get every night?	
4. What kind of healthy food do you like or dislike?	
5. What do you think the ideal routine for staying healthy is?	
6. What's your routine when you arrive in class?	
7. What's your afternoon and evening routine?	
8. Can you tell me a recipe for a healthy drink or dish?	
9. How often do you exercise?	
10. What are your unhealthy habits?	

Word Bank

Check (✔) the words that you know. If there are any words that you don't know, look them up in your dictionary.

Useful Phrases

- [ ] It sounds healthy.
- [ ] You can do it.
- [ ] I'm supposed to …
- [ ] I get accustomed to …
- [ ] ten to six
- [ ] five past seven
- [ ] half an hour
- [ ] a half package of tofu
- [ ] one third of a cup
- [ ] one slice of bread
- [ ] a tablespoon of honey
- [ ] 36 degrees Celsius
- [ ] for my health
- [ ] on weekdays
- [ ] right now
- [ ] per day
- [ ] at least
- [ ] on top
- [ ] to be honest

Nouns

- [ ] population
- [ ] average body temperature
- [ ] energy
- [ ] diet
- [ ] routine
- [ ] morning person
- [ ] athlete
- [ ] full marathon
- [ ] home gym
- [ ] court
- [ ] yoga mattress
- [ ] sweat suit
- [ ] medicine

- [ ] light breakfast
- [ ] food supply
- [ ] groceries
- [ ] recipe
- [ ] ingredient
- [ ] mixture
- [ ] shellfish
- [ ] lettuce
- [ ] celery
- [ ] blueberry
- [ ] peanut butter
- [ ] plain yogurt
- [ ] power drink
- [ ] soy milk
- [ ] ice cube
- [ ] freezer
- [ ] blender
- [ ] bowl
- [ ] plate

Verbs

- [ ] be careful about *something*
- [ ] be in great shape
- [ ] stay healthy
- [ ] weigh
- [ ] gain weight
- [ ] lose weight
- [ ] take in 1,800 kilocalories
- [ ] go for a run
- [ ] walk a dog
- [ ] take a sauna
- [ ] cool down
- [ ] take a nap
- [ ] skip breakfast
- [ ] check e-mail
- [ ] leave home

- [ ] arrive in class
- [ ] practice *something*
- [ ] do a push-up
- [ ] do a sit-up
- [ ] do stretching exercises
- [ ] do weight training
- [ ] hit balls around
- [ ] give instructions
- [ ] describe
- [ ] prepare
- [ ] take out *something*
- [ ] cut up
- [ ] cut *something* into thin slices
- [ ] slice up
- [ ] add
- [ ] pour
- [ ] mix
- [ ] put
- [ ] match

Adjectives

- [ ] professional
- [ ] amateur
- [ ] perfect
- [ ] ideal
- [ ] typical
- [ ] long-distance
- [ ] tiring
- [ ] fresh
- [ ] frozen

Adverbs and Prepositions

- [ ] extremely
- [ ] easily

Review for Units 7-9

🔊 *Speak Out 1* **Fill in the blanks with the words in the boxes. Use capitalization when necessary. Then, read the conversations with your partner.**

1
A: _____ me. _____ you tell me where the Sky Hotel is, please?

B: Of _____. It's just _____ this street on the right.

A: Down this street on the _____?

B: That's right. It's _____ Joe's Pizza and the Sun Bank.

A: I think I got it. And one more thing. _____ is the City Mall? Is it _____ the hotel?

B: Yes, it's _____ the street from the hotel. You can't miss it.

A: Thank you.

B: No _____.

could	across	where	problem	between	course	right	excuse	near	down

2
A: What _____ of movies do you like?

B: I love _____ movies.

A: Do you _____ to see the new Harry Potter movie tonight?

B: Sure.

A: Okay. _____ call the cinema.

(Making a phone call)

C: Century Cinema. _____ I help you?

A: Yes. _____ you tell me _____ Harry Potter is playing tonight?

C: _____. It starts at 7:20 and 9:45.

A: Okay. _____ you very much.

C: You're welcome. Have a good day.

want	I'll	may	fantasy	could	what time	thank	sure	kind

3

A: _____ the new book that you're reading?

B: It's _____ good. It's _____ morning routines.

A: Sounds interesting. So _____ your morning routine?

B: Well, I'm quite strict about my morning routine. I _____ early … um … usually at 5:30. _____, I wash my face. Next, I have a glass of water _____ I do some stretching. _____, I go for a short run and then I have fruit and toast for breakfast. _____, I take a shower and then leave for school. That's a _____ morning for me.

A: Sounds tiring.

| pretty   after that   get up   what's   finally   how's   typical   about   first   and then |

🔊 *Speak Out 2* **Talk about one of the topics. Keep the talk going for at least 1 minute.**

| travel in Japan | music | J-pop | movies | books | health |

| food | manga | video games | travel abroad |

| your evening routine | your routine at school |

🔊 *Speak Out 3* **Talk about one of the topics. Keep the talk going for at least 2 minutes.**

| the best place to visit in Japan | your favorite kind of sports |

| how to make a food dish or drink | how to make a healthy salad |

| what you do to stay healthy | what you like to read or watch |

 **Speak Out 4** **Make a short presentation about one of the topics. Refer to the format and example phrases in the box when you prepare.**

• Your best trip • Your favorite way to travel and why

• Problems you had when traveling and why • Your favorite Japanese city

• Places you have visited in Japan

Introduction	Hello everyone. Today, I'm going to talk about my best trip.
General Feeling / Main Idea	My favorite trip was to Los Angeles in the United States. It was my first trip abroad and I was so excited.
Details	I went to L.A. when I was in junior high school. I went with my … During the trip, I saw … On the first day, we arrived in L.A. … On the second day, we … On the other days, we … On the final day, we decided to …
Conclusion	When we got home, we were tired but very satisfied.
Summary	So far, it was the best trip of my life. I want to go there again soon.

 **Speak Out 5** **Ask your partner the questions. Always answer with at least two sentences and continue the conversation with follow-up questions.**

1. Where is the nearest convenience store?
2. Could you tell me where the library is?
3. Do you know how to get to the station from here?
4. Where have you traveled abroad?
5. Where have you traveled in Japan?
6. What is the most interesting place that you've traveled to?
7. What is your favorite Japanese place to visit? Why?
8. Do you like watching TV?
9. What kind of movies or TV shows do you like watching?
10. What kind of video or phone games do you like?
11. What kind of music do you like?
12. What's your morning routine?
13. What's your routine before you go to bed?
14. Are you careful about what you eat?
15. How long do you sleep on weekdays?

Listen In 1 Listen to the conversations and answer the questions.

B
39-44

1. **a)** Where is Victoria Park? _____

   b) Where is the bakery? _____

2. **a)** What street is the National Art Museum on? _____

   b) Which will the tourist see first, the Civic Tower or the National
   Art Museum? _____

3. **a)** What are the store's opening and closing hours? _____

   b) What are the store's opening and closing hours on the weekend? _____

4. **a)** How long is the roller coaster and how long does it take? _____

   b) How fast does the roller coaster travel? _____

5. **a)** What three things does the singing club do at its meetings? _____

   b) What time and what days does the singing club meet? _____

6. **a)** What ingredients are needed for this drink? _____

   b) What are the first two ingredients to put in the blender? _____

Listen In 2 Listen to the conversations and read the statements.
Circle T for true and F for false. Correct the false statements.

B
45-50

1. **a)** The post office is very close to the speakers. T / F

   b) The restaurant is close to the post office. T / F

2. **a)** The Grand Hotel is in the park. T / F

   b) The hotel is on the left of a blue building. T / F

3. **a)** Tickets cost either 28 dollars or 15 dollars. T / F

   b) Children under four get in free. T / F

4. **a)** Both speakers like anime with princes and princesses. T / F

   b) Both speakers have seen the anime *Zoombies*. T / F

5. **a)** The man wakes up and then takes a shower. T / F

   b) The man has lunch but not breakfast. T / F

6. **a)** The ingredients for this drink are orange juice, one banana and ice cubes. T / F

   b) The drink should be used for breakfast only. T / F

People I Know

Read the conversations with your partner. Then, make new conversations using the words in the boxes.

A: My best friend is really kind. Yesterday, I was very sick and she cooked me dinner.

B: That's great. Do I know her?

A: She's standing over there. She has long blonde hair and she's thin.

B: Is she wearing glasses?

A: Yeah.

B: I think she's in my class.

short curly hair kind of tall a blue dress	
dark hair quite pretty a hat	

A: What does your brother look like?

B: Well, he's extremely tall, slim, and kind of handsome.

A: What's he like?

B: He's very nice.

A: He's just like you!

B: He's smarter and more fashionable than I am.

A: Really? I want to meet him someday.

average height, chubby, and sort of cute outgoing funnier and more talkative than	
short, bald, and muscular quiet more serious and not as funny as	

73

Describing People

Look at the phrases for describing people. Listen and repeat.

Describing Build	She's short. She's average height. She's tall. He's thin and fit. He has an average build. He's muscular. He looks athletic. He's chubby and out of shape. He's overweight.
Describing Hair and Face	She has long straight hair. She has medium-length hair. She has short curly hair. She has dark hair. She has dyed hair. He has gray hair. He's bald. He has a shaved head. He has a beard. He has a moustache. She wears glasses. She's cute. She's pretty. He's good-looking. He's handsome.
Describing Clothes	She's wearing a black sweater. She's wearing a polka-dot skirt. He's wearing a blue shirt. He's wearing a white jacket and jeans.

 Listen to the conversations. Who are the speakers talking about? Put the number of the conversation in the correct box.

 Describe the people below to your partner.

1. Some of the people in your family
2. Some of your good friends
3. Some famous people that you admire
4. Some of your teachers and classmates

Speaking Strategy

Emphasizing

When you want to change the nuance of adjectives, you can use phrases for emphasizing. Listen and repeat.

B 58

Affirmative	• He's a little rude. • She's kind of lazy.
	• He's sort of hardworking. • He's nice.
	• He's quite talkative. • She's pretty quiet.
	• They are very shy. • They are so negative.
	• They are extremely friendly.
Negative	• He's not strict. • He's not very positive.
	• They are not so serious. • She's not interesting at all.

◁)) Speak Out 1   **Fill in the blanks. Then, read the sentences to your partner.**

1 Let me tell you about some of the people I know. One of my best

friends is _____. He/She is _____ quiet and

(name)

very _____. Another friend who I like is _____

(name)

and he/she is _____ talkative. I think my friends

are _____.

2 As for my family, my father is _____ strict, and my mother is _____ supportive.

The other members in my family are _____. As for myself, I

think I'm not so _____ but I am really _____.

◁)) Speak Out 2   **Ask your partner the questions. Use phrases for emphasizing when you answer.**

1. Can you tell me about your best friend?   → Well, my best friend is extremely …
2. Can you tell me about your favorite teacher?   → My favorite teacher is really …
3. Can you tell me about your family?   → First, my father is quite … and my mother is …
4. What kind of people do you like?   → I like people who are very … and …
5. What kind of people do you dislike?   → I dislike people who are not … and who are …

Describing Personality

Look at the phrases for describing personality. Listen and repeat.

What's she like?	→ She's outgoing.
What kind of person is he?	→ He's very dull.
Who is funnier, your mother or your father?	→ My mother is funnier than my father.
Who is more talkative, you or your best friend?	→ My best friend is more talkative than I am.
Who is the coolest person you know?	→ The coolest person I know is Aya.
Are you the most fashionable among your friends?	→ No, I'm not. Jim is the most fashionable.

Note: cool–cooler–the coolest / fashionable–more fashionable–the most fashionable

Listen In   Listen to the conversations and complete the sentences.

1. Dave is _____ and very _____. He is _____ energetic and _____ than the other guys in class.

2. Alice is kind of _____ but she is the _____ girl in class. Linda used to be kind of _____, but now she is _____ positive. She is _____ than Alice.

3. Kim is the _____ student in class, but she is extremely _____. Paul is very _____ and _____. Mark is so _____ and _____. He is also really _____.

Speak Out   Fill in the blanks with the words in the box. Change the ending of words when necessary. Then, ask your partner the questions.

friendly   polite   kind   fashionable   positive   negative   smart   stupid   dull   funny   serious
quiet   talkative   interesting   mean   shy   outgoing   easygoing   hardworking   lazy   strict

1. Who is _____, your mom or your dad?   → I think my … is …

2. Who is more _____, you or your best friend?   → Well, … is more …

3. Do you think you're more _____ than I am?   → I guess that …

4. Who is the _____ person you know?   → Maybe … is the … person.

5. Who is the most _____ in your family?   → I'm sure that … is the most …

6. Who do you think is the most _____ in class?   → I think … is the most …

WRAP IT UP

Write your answers to the questions. Then, ask your partner the questions. Use phrases for emphasizing when you answer.

Example
A: Can you describe one of our classmates?
B: Well, he has short dyed hair and wears glasses. He's kind of tall and good-looking. He's smart, too.
A: That must be Shun! I think he's funny.

Questions	Your answers	Your partner's answers
1. What does one of our classmates look like? What are they like?		
2. What does your favorite actor or musician look like?		
3. What do you look like?		
4. What kind of person is your best friend?		
5. What does your teacher look like?		
6. What kind of person do you want to get married to?		
7. Can you tell me about the funniest person you know?		
8. What kind of people are you not attracted to? Why?		
9. Can you describe your own personality?		
10. Can you describe one of your family members?		

Word Bank

Check (✔) the words that you know. If there are any words that you don't know, look them up in your dictionary.

Useful Phrases

- [ ] Which one?
- [ ] He's just like you.
- [ ] She's a lot of fun.
- [ ] I wish I could …
- [ ] when necessary
- [ ] at the beginning
- [ ] by the window
- [ ] over there

Nouns

- [ ] rugby
- [ ] school band
- [ ] head cheerleader
- [ ] exchange student
- [ ] guy
- [ ] shaved head
- [ ] beard
- [ ] moustache
- [ ] clothes
- [ ] jacket
- [ ] sweater
- [ ] shirt
- [ ] skirt
- [ ] jeans
- [ ] glasses
- [ ] personality
- [ ] grade

Verbs

- [ ] be out of shape
- [ ] be best friends
- [ ] get along with *someone*
- [ ] make *someone* laugh

- [ ] stand alone
- [ ] wear
- [ ] share
- [ ] emphasize

Adjectives

- [ ] short
- [ ] average height
- [ ] tall
- [ ] thin
- [ ] fit
- [ ] average build
- [ ] athletic
- [ ] muscular
- [ ] chubby
- [ ] fat
- [ ] overweight
- [ ] medium-length
- [ ] long
- [ ] straight
- [ ] curly
- [ ] dark
- [ ] blonde
- [ ] gray
- [ ] bald
- [ ] cute
- [ ] pretty
- [ ] beautiful
- [ ] good-looking
- [ ] handsome
- [ ] cool
- [ ] fashionable
- [ ] nice
- [ ] energetic
- [ ] positive
- [ ] negative

- [ ] supportive
- [ ] kind
- [ ] friendly
- [ ] mean
- [ ] outgoing
- [ ] shy
- [ ] talkative
- [ ] quiet
- [ ] hardworking
- [ ] lazy
- [ ] polite
- [ ] impolite
- [ ] rude
- [ ] interesting
- [ ] boring
- [ ] strict
- [ ] serious
- [ ] easygoing
- [ ] funny
- [ ] dull
- [ ] smart
- [ ] stupid
- [ ] sick
- [ ] polka-dot

Adverbs and Prepositions

- [ ] extremely
- [ ] very
- [ ] really
- [ ] kind of
- [ ] sort of
- [ ] not very …
- [ ] not so …
- [ ] not … at all

Storytelling

Read the conversations with your partner. Then, make new conversations using the words in the boxes.

A: You'll never believe what happened.
B: What?
A: I went to visit my aunt in Tochigi last week, and while I was sleeping on the train, someone stole my wallet.
B: No kidding.
A: Luckily, someone returned it later.
B: Was your money still inside?
A: Unfortunately not!

Oh, no!	Fortunately,
Really?	I was lucky because

2
A: Did I tell you what happened yesterday?
B: No. What happened?
A: I had some French fries for lunch. While I was giving a presentation in class, some classmates started laughing at me.
B: Why was that?
A: I had ketchup on my shirt.
B: Really? How did you feel?
A: I felt so embarrassed.

two French fries in my pocket It was embarrassing.
ketchup on my collar I was so embarrassed.

Past Tense Questions and Answers

Look at the use of the past tense questions and answers to tell a story. Listen and repeat.

A: What happened?   B: Someone stole my passport from my bag.

A: What were you doing at the time?   B: I was shopping for clothes downtown.

A: How did it happen?   B: One man was asking me for directions and another
                                               man stole my passport.

A: What happened then?   B: They ran away and then I called the police.

A: What happened in the end?   B: The police found the two men and my passport.

 **Listen to the conversations and read the statements. Circle T for true and F for false. Correct the false statements.**

1. While students were taking a test, the teacher broke a computer.   T / F

2. The man got married in Las Vegas.   T / F

3. The woman broke her phone and hurt her arm.   T / F

4. While driving through the mountains, the man hit two deer.   T / F

5. Two dogs ran after the woman and bit her.   T / F

 **Change the verbs to be past progressive or past tense. Then, read the sentences to your partner.**

1. I (see) _____ a cockroach and (fall) _____ down while I (wash) _____ my hair.

2. I (drop) _____ my bag and (lose) _____ it while I (ride) _____ my bike.

3. A monkey (bite) _____ my sister while we (walk) _____ in the woods.

4. He (scratch) _____ his arm while he (sleep) _____.

5. While I (do) _____ my homework, my computer (break) _____ down.

6. I (go) _____ to visit my grandmother, and while we (clean) _____
   her apartment, I (find) _____ an old photo album.

7. While we (take) _____ a test, my cellphone (ring) _____
   and my teacher (get) _____ very angry.

8. While she (study) _____ in her room, someone
   (come) _____ and (leave) _____ flowers at the door.

Reacting to Events in a Story

When you want to know more about another person's story, you can use phrases for reacting to events in a story. Listen and repeat.

B
69

- How did you feel?   → I felt excited.
- What did you think?   → I was excited.
- How was it?   → It was exciting.
- You must have been embarrassed. → Yes, I was.
- It must have been embarrassing. → No, it wasn't. There was no one around me at the time.

 **Speak Out 1** Circle the correct words and complete the conversation. Then, read the conversation with your partner.

A: Did I tell you what happened last night?

B: No. What happened?

A: My mother told me that she was extremely [disappointed / disappointing] because I hadn't done any housework recently. Then, she started crying.

B: You're kidding. How did you feel?

A: It was so [shocked / shocking]. I've never seen my mother cry. I told her that I was sorry and I would help more often. She was [pleased / pleasing] to hear that.

B: That's good. Anyway, I have an interesting story, too. I went to an [excited / exciting] baseball game yesterday, and a home run ball almost hit me. I was so [surprised / surprising].

A: You must have been [scared / scary].

B: Oh yeah, but it was [disappointed / disappointing] that I didn't get the ball.

 **Speak Out 2** Read the sentences to your partner. Use phrases for reacting to events when you respond.

1. While I was typing, my computer broke down.   → How did you feel?
2. I saw the Carnival while I was visiting Brazil.   → How was it?
3. While we were traveling in the States, we saw the Grand Canyon. → What did you think?
4. While I was walking my dog, my shoes came off and I fell down. → It must have been …
5. My teacher gave me an A for my report.   → You must have been …

Telling Stories

Look at the questions and answers for telling stories. Listen and repeat.

Did I ever tell you my scary story?	→ No, I don't think so.
Have I told you my camping story?	→ No, you haven't.
When did it happen?	→ It was when I was in kindergarten and I was five years old.
What happened?	→ My family went camping in Nagano.
What happened then?	→ I decided to play in the forest by myself, and then I got lost.
What happened in the end?	→ The police found me three hours later.
Were you frightened?	→ Yes, it was very frightening.

Listen In Listen to the conversations and complete the summaries.

1. The man was _____ years old when the story happened. While he and his brother were in the woods, they _____ a bee's nest and started _____ stones. When the boy _____ it, the bees started attacking them, and finally he _____ stung. In the end, he had to stay in bed for two _____.

2. The story is about the man's _____. One day, a vacuum cleaner saleswoman _____ to the door and his mom _____ her to vacuum the _____ house. She did it, but his mom _____ buy the vacuum. She invited the saleswoman to _____ instead. In the end, they _____ friends.

Speak Out Fill in the blanks. Then, read the conversation with your partner.

A: Did I ever tell you my funny story?

B: No, I don't think so. When _____?

A: It was when I was in _____ school and I was _____ years old. While I was traveling in Nara with my _____, I gave a foreigner wrong directions to a temple.

B: What happened then?

A: Later, he saw me and got very angry at me.

B: Oh, no. You must have been _____.

A: Definitely. It was _____.

WRAP IT UP

Think of two stories and write notes in the boxes. Then, tell the stories to your partner. The stories do not have to be true.

Example
A: Did I ever tell you my embarrassing story?
B: No, I don't think so. When did it happen?
A: Well, it happened when I was in junior high school and I was 14 years old. We were playing volleyball in the school gym.
B: What happened then?
A: I hit a hard serve and it hit the teacher in the face. His nose started bleeding and he had to go to the hospital. In the end, we found out that his nose was broken.
B: Oh, no! You must have been shocked.
A: Absolutely. I felt really sorry for him.

Story 1	
When did it happen?	
How old were you at the time?	
Where did it happen?	
What was happening at the time?	
What happened then?	
How did you feel?	

Story 2	
When did it happen?	
How old were you at the time?	
Where did it happen?	
What was happening at the time?	
What happened then?	
How did you feel?	

Word Bank

Check (✔) the words that you know. If there are any words that you don't know, look them up in your dictionary.

Useful Phrases

- [ ] No kidding.
- [ ] Congratulations.
- [ ] She's happy to hear that.
- [ ] Luckily, …
- [ ] Fortunately, …
- [ ] Unfortunately, …
- [ ] before going to school
- [ ] at the time
- [ ] in the end
- [ ] in the woods
- [ ] a bunch of flowers

Nouns

- [ ] event
- [ ] animal park
- [ ] school gym
- [ ] hard serve
- [ ] home run ball
- [ ] damage
- [ ] cockroach
- [ ] bee
- [ ] deer
- [ ] forest
- [ ] nest
- [ ] pole
- [ ] sticker
- [ ] wallet
- [ ] passport
- [ ] vacuum cleaner
- [ ] saleswoman
- [ ] foreigner
- [ ] ketchup

Verbs

- [ ] attack
- [ ] bite
- [ ] scratch
- [ ] throw
- [ ] hit
- [ ] break a computer
- [ ] break down
- [ ] knock *something* over
- [ ] get stung
- [ ] bleed
- [ ] stay in bed
- [ ] run away
- [ ] run after *someone*
- [ ] follow
- [ ] come to the door
- [ ] come up to *something*
- [ ] walk around the town
- [ ] give wrong directions
- [ ] get lost
- [ ] get stuck
- [ ] go off the road
- [ ] come off
- [ ] drop
- [ ] look for *something*
- [ ] return
- [ ] find out
- [ ] notice
- [ ] yell
- [ ] get angry
- [ ] laugh at *someone*
- [ ] feel sorry for *someone*
- [ ] think of *something*
- [ ] change *one's* clothes
- [ ] vacuum the whole house
- [ ] invite *someone* to dinner

- [ ] become friends
- [ ] believe
- [ ] get a job as a cook
- [ ] give a presentation
- [ ] tell a story
- [ ] type
- [ ] ring
- [ ] cancel

Adjectives

- [ ] excited
- [ ] exciting
- [ ] surprised
- [ ] surprising
- [ ] shocked
- [ ] shocking
- [ ] frightened
- [ ] frightening
- [ ] scared
- [ ] scary
- [ ] embarrassed
- [ ] embarrassing
- [ ] disappointed
- [ ] disappointing
- [ ] bored
- [ ] boring

Adverbs and Prepositions

- [ ] later
- [ ] then
- [ ] around
- [ ] through
- [ ] safely
- [ ] instead
- [ ] anymore

Society

Read the conversations with your partner. Then, make new conversations using the words in the boxes.

1
A: Do you have a few minutes? I need your advice.
B: Sure. What happened?
A: My neighbor's dog keeps barking all night and it really annoys me. What do you suggest I do?
B: I think you should go over and complain.
A: I don't think that would work.
B: Well, then, why don't you talk to the landlord?
A: That might work.

What should I do?   how about talking
That's a good idea.

What do you think I should do?
if I were you, I would talk
That's not such a good idea.

2
A: How do you feel about global warming?
B: I definitely think that we should do something as soon as possible.
A: Personally, I think we should reduce our use of fossil fuels.
B: I agree. I feel that we should use more electric vehicles.
A: Yes. I think electric cars are a great idea.
B: Nowadays, technology should help us fight global warming.

What do you think of
In my opinion,   I totally agree.

What's your opinion of
I definitely think   I think so, too.

Asking for and Giving Advice

Look at the phrases for asking for and giving advice. Listen and repeat.

Asking for Advice	What should I do? What do you think I should do?
	What do you suggest I do? I need your advice.
Giving Advice	I think you should complain to your neighbor.
	Why don't you write a complaint to your local politician?
	How about talking to the owner? If I were you, I would call the police.
Responding to Advice	That's a good idea. That might work. That's not such a good idea.
	I don't think that would work.

 **Listen to the conversations and read the statements. Circle T for true and F for false. Correct the false statements.**

1. The woman will probably go over and complain to the neighbor.   T / F
2. The woman suggests that the student who is being bullied talk to the teacher.   T / F
3. The woman thinks her boyfriend has "nomophobia."   T / F
4. The man will probably look for a new roommate.   T / F
5. The man suggests that the woman take her parents to Africa.   T / F

 **Read the conversation. Then, talk about solutions for each situation.**

A: There are a lot of crows that go through our garbage bags. What should I do?

B: Well, if I were you, I would write a complaint to your local politician.

A: That's a good idea. Do you have any other advice?

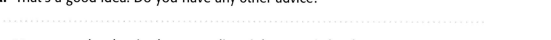

1. My younger brother is always reading violent comic books.
2. My neighbor has a dog that barks all the time.
3. Some dogs go to the washroom on the street and the owners don't clean up.
4. One of my friends is being bullied at work by her co-workers.
5. Many people are leaving their trash in the park.
6. I'm angry because my friend always checks her phone while we're eating.

Expressing Opinions

When you discuss issues, it is important to express your opinions. Listen and repeat.

Expressing Opinions	I think we should teach children English at a very young age. I definitely feel that the government shouldn't waste our money. Personally, I think online bullies should be punished more severely. In my opinion, we should stop destroying the rainforests.
Agreeing and Disagreeing	I guess so. I kind of agree. I agree. I totally agree. I think so, too. I kind of disagree. I disagree. I don't agree. I'm sorry but I don't agree. To be honest, I totally disagree.

Speak Out Fill in the blanks with the words in the box. Then, read the conversations with your partner.

agree   should   shouldn't   let   stop   think   stopped   allowed   good   feel   phones   too

1 **A:** How do you feel about video games?

B: I think they're not _____ for children. We shouldn't _____ young children play video games.

A: I'm sorry but I don't _____. In my opinion, video games are good for developing children's minds.

2 **A:** What do you think of students who are always checking their _____ in class?

B: I definitely think that students should be _____.

A: I agree. I think that students shouldn't be _____ to bring their cellphones to school.

3 **A:** How do you _____ about Japanese anime?

B: I think they are amazing.

A: I think so, _____.

4 **A:** What do you _____ of people who throw garbage on the streets?

B: I think that they should _____ doing that.

A: I totally agree. Personally, I think they _____ be fined.

B: Yes, we _____ make our streets so dirty.

Discussing Issues

Look at the phrases for discussing issues. Listen and repeat.

Bringing Up Issues	Recently, there have been many parents who abuse their own children.
	Nowadays, many young people don't work and just stay at home.
	I'm worried about deforestation around the world.
Asking for Opinions	What do you think of disposable chopsticks?
	How do you feel about bullying at school?
Expressing Uncertainty	I don't know what to say. That's a difficult question.
	I'm not sure about that. I don't know very much about that issue.

 Listen to the conversations and read the statements. Circle T for true and F for false. Correct the false statements.

1. The man thinks that it is okay to have vending machines in schools.   T / F

2. Both speakers are happy with the new highway.   T / F

3. Both speakers think that parents don't read enough books to their children.   T / F

4. The woman doesn't think all plastic should be banned.   T / F

5. The man believes that there should be no consumption tax.   T / F

6. Both speakers think that people should plant more trees.   T / F

7. The man thinks that magazines shouldn't show any photos that are taken in public spaces.   T / F

 Ask your partner the questions and discuss.

1. Recently, online bullying has increased. What do you think?

2. Nowadays, we see a lot of TV programs about competitive eating. How do you feel about that?

3. I'm worried about children who eat meals alone at home. What do you think?

4. What do you think of your English education so far?

5. How do you feel about zoos?

6. What do you think of disposable chopsticks?

WRAP IT UP

Discuss social and global issues with your partner. Use phrases for asking for and giving advice, and expressing opinions.

Example
A: How do you feel about your neighbors?
B: They're okay, but recently, my neighbor bought a violin and the sound annoys me. What should I do?
A: Well, I think you should complain to the landlord.
B: That's a good idea.

Example
A: Nowadays, many people are shopping online. What do you think?
B: Personally, I think it's very convenient and fun.
A: I disagree. I prefer to shop in stores and see and touch the things I want to buy.

Example
A: What do you think of plastic bags given out at some stores?
B: That's a difficult question. Well, personally, I think they're not needed.
A: I agree. In my opinion, we should carry our own bags when we go out.
B: I strongly agree.

neighbors	the Internet	disposable chopsticks	alcohol
noise pollution	child abuse	single-use plastic	minimum income
garbage	bullying	recycling	online shopping
pandemics	food waste	whaling	vending machines
zoos	climate change	space travel	smartphones
education	travel	vegetarianism	video games
aging society	deforestation	self-driving cars	violent comic books
young people	mental health issues	social media	AI

Word Bank

Check (✔) the words that you know. If there are any words that you don't know, look them up in your dictionary.

Useful Phrases

- [ ] It's a waste of money.
- [ ] … and things like that
- [ ] as soon as possible
- [ ] at a very young age
- [ ] all night

Nouns

- [ ] society
- [ ] human
- [ ] government
- [ ] public worker
- [ ] co-worker
- [ ] landlord
- [ ] owner
- [ ] neighbor
- [ ] roommate
- [ ] private life
- [ ] rule
- [ ] culture
- [ ] education
- [ ] bullying
- [ ] child abuse
- [ ] violence
- [ ] documentary
- [ ] issue
- [ ] complaint
- [ ] advice
- [ ] solution
- [ ] volunteer
- [ ] recycling
- [ ] global warming
- [ ] rainforest
- [ ] deforestation
- [ ] fossil fuels

- [ ] climate change
- [ ] minimum income
- [ ] vegetarianism
- [ ] racism
- [ ] aging society
- [ ] endangered species
- [ ] whaling
- [ ] environmental problem
- [ ] crow
- [ ] garbage
- [ ] trash
- [ ] food waste
- [ ] disposable chopsticks
- [ ] plastic bag
- [ ] single-use plastic
- [ ] grocery store
- [ ] vending machine
- [ ] soft drink
- [ ] junk food
- [ ] competitive eating
- [ ] drunk driver
- [ ] cigarette smoking
- [ ] smell
- [ ] air pollution
- [ ] hybrid car
- [ ] sidewalk
- [ ] public transportation
- [ ] washing machine
- [ ] electricity
- [ ] health insurance

Verbs

- [ ] be interested in *something*
- [ ] be worried about *something*
- [ ] be angry with *someone*
- [ ] take *someone*'s photo

- [ ] go to the washroom
- [ ] bark
- [ ] annoy
- [ ] bother
- [ ] bully
- [ ] abuse
- [ ] harm
- [ ] hunt
- [ ] cut down
- [ ] reduce
- [ ] destroy
- [ ] waste
- [ ] solve
- [ ] suggest
- [ ] go over
- [ ] complain
- [ ] take away
- [ ] punish
- [ ] ban
- [ ] store
- [ ] build
- [ ] develop
- [ ] plant

Adjectives

- [ ] illegal
- [ ] violent
- [ ] local

Adverbs and Prepositions

- [ ] totally
- [ ] severely
- [ ] foolishly
- [ ] already

🔊 *Speak Out 1* **Fill in the blanks with the words in the boxes. Use capitalization when necessary. Then, read the conversations with your partner.**

1

A: Hey, look! There's Jeff Jones. He's on the basketball team. He's _____ cute.

B: _____ one is he? What does he _____ like?

A: _____ really tall and _____ short dark hair.

B: Oh, yeah, I see him. _____ wearing a red sweater?

A: Yes. He's so _____ … and he's cool.

B: And that's Jeff's girlfriend there.

A: Oh, no! Don't tell me he has a girlfriend.

B: Yes, _____. She has long _____ hair. _____ wearing a blue dress.

A: What's she _____?

B: She's the opposite of Jeff. She's actually quite quiet.

athletic	he does	like	look	so	which	he's	has	is he	blonde	she's

2

A: _____ I tell you what happened today?

B: No. What _____?

A: While we _____ taking a test, the fire alarm _____ off.

B: You're _____. What happened _____?

A: We went outside the classroom and we _____ return until the end of class.

B: So what happened _____?

A: _____, the teacher canceled the test.

B: You were _____!

happened	went	kidding	lucky	couldn't	did	then	in the end	were	fortunately

3

A: I love reading books.

B: Me, _____.

A: _____, young people are not reading books anymore. It's _____.

B: I _____. But I _____ that people are reading stuff on their phones or on the Internet.

A: That's _____. It's sad that people are reading less and less.

B: I _____ agree. I feel reading is so important for learning new things.

A: You're _____. Oh, that reminds me. My friend Jim keeps borrowing my books but he doesn't return them until about one year later. What do you think I _____ do?

B: Well, if I _____ you, I _____ only give him one book at a time.

A: That might _____. I'll try it.

> think   shocking   right   would   too   work
> nowadays   were   agree   totally   true   should

 **Speak Out 2**   **Talk about one of the topics. Keep the talk going for at least 1 minute.**

vending machines	books	endangered species	hunting animals

pets	zoos	deforestation	global warming	violent video games

disposable chopsticks	plastic	bicycles	paper waste

hybrid cars	anime	manga	senior citizens	air pollution

the Internet	poverty	SNS	robots	children

English education	junk food	foreigners	pop music	jazz music

 *Speak Out 3* **Think of a personal story and talk about one of the topics. Refer to the format and example phrases in the box when you prepare.**

- A family story   • A funny story   • An embarrassing story
- A scary story   • A memorable story or experience   • A story about an accomplishment
- An interesting story that happened to someone else

Introduction	Hi everyone. Today, I'd like to share a story with you.
Background	This is a scary story that happened to me when I was about five years old. I was staying with my grandmother at the time.
Details	One night, I went to bed early. Then, … After that, …
Conclusion	In the end, I realized that my grandmother …
Summary	I was so scared that night. I will never forget it.

 *Speak Out 4* **Ask your partner the questions. Always answer with at least two sentences and continue the conversation with follow-up questions.**

1. What does your best friend look like?
2. What are your parents like?
3. Can you describe one of famous people that you admire?
4. Who is the coolest person you know?
5. Can you describe one of your classmates?
6. Can you describe the teacher's clothes?
7. Do you have any good train stories?
8. Have you ever been embarrassed in class?
9. Could you tell us a story about a time when you won or lost something?
10. My younger brother is always on his phone, even at dinner time. What do you recommend I do?
11. I want to be healthier. What do you think I should do?
12. I want to be a better English speaker. What do you suggest I do?
13. What do you think of the environmental problems we face today?
14. What's your opinion of people who walk and check their phones at the same time?
15. What's your opinion of vending machines that sell junk food or drinks?

Listen In 1   **Listen to the conversations and answer the questions.**   B 88-93

1. **a)** What does the English teacher look like?   _____

   b) What is the English teacher like?   _____

2. **a)** What does Alice look like?   _____

   b) What is Alice like?   _____

3. **a)** What happened to the woman?   _____

   b) Can the woman still drive her parents' car?   _____

4. **a)** What was the woman doing with her sister?   _____

   b) Why did the woman go to the hospital?   _____

5. **a)** What is the man concerned about?   _____

   b) What two pieces of advice does the woman give?   _____

6. **a)** Why did the school ban vending machines?   _____

   b) Do both speakers agree with the school?   _____

Listen In 2   **Listen to the conversations and read the statements.**
Circle T for true and F for false. Correct the false statements.   B 94-99

1. **a)** The man's sister is taller than he is.   T / F

   b) The man's sister is playing the piano.   T / F

2. **a)** Takako is shorter than Kelly.   T / F

   b) Takako is not as smart as Kelly.   T / F

3. **a)** Last night, two dogs chased the woman and bit her.   T / F

   b) The woman yelled at the two dogs and they ran away.   T / F

4. **a)** The story happened when the man's father was in high school.   T / F

   b) The man's father spilled white paint on him.   T / F

5. **a)** The woman is interested in cooking.   T / F

   b) The man recommends that the woman read books about cooking.   T / F

6. **a)** The speakers are talking mainly about the loss of forests.   T / F

   b) Some forests are being cut down to make palm oil for cooking.   T / F

Common Regular Verbs

Base Form	Simple Past	Base Form	Simple Past	Base Form	Simple Past
work	work**ed**	play	play**ed**	happen	happen**ed**
walk	walk**ed**	enjoy	enjoy**ed**	open	open**ed**
live	live**d**	drop	drop**ped**	prefer	prefer**red**
dance	dance**d**	hug	hug**ged**	admit	admit**ted**
study	stud**ied**	show	show**ed**		
cry	cr**ied**	relax	relax**ed**		

Common Irregular Verbs

Base Form	Simple Past	Past Participle	Base Form	Simple Past	Past Participle
be (is/am/are)	was/were	been	keep	kept	kept
become	became	become	know	knew	known
begin	began	begun	lead	led	led
bend	bent	bent	leave	left	left
bite	bit	bitten	lose	lost	lost
blow	blew	blown	make	made	made
break	broke	broken	meet	met	met
bring	brought	brought	pay	paid	paid
build	built	built	put	put	put
buy	bought	bought	quit	quit	quit
catch	caught	caught	read	read	read
choose	chose	chosen	ride	rode	ridden
come	came	come	run	ran	run
cost	cost	cost	say	said	said
cut	cut	cut	see	saw	seen
do	did	done	sell	sold	sold
draw	drew	drawn	send	sent	sent
drink	drank	drunk	shake	shook	shaken
drive	drove	driven	shoot	shot	shot
eat	ate	eaten	sing	sang	sung
fall	fell	fallen	sit	sat	sat
feed	fed	fed	sleep	slept	slept
feel	felt	felt	speak	spoke	spoken
fight	fought	fought	spend	spent	spent
find	found	found	stand	stood	stood
fly	flew	flown	steal	stole	stolen
forget	forgot	forgotten	swim	swam	swum
get	got	gotten	take	took	taken
give	gave	given	teach	taught	taught
go	went	gone	tear	tore	torn
grow	grew	grown	tell	told	told
hang	hung	hung	think	thought	thought
have	had	had	throw	threw	thrown
hear	heard	heard	understand	understood	understood
hide	hid	hidden	wake	woke	woken
hit	hit	hit	wear	wore	worn
hold	held	held	win	won	won
hurt	hurt	hurt	write	wrote	written

クラス用音声CD有り（別売）

Take It Easy! Second Edition
Talking Naturally and Confidently

2008年3月20日　初版発行
2021年1月20日　第2版発行
2024年1月20日　第2版第4刷

著　者　Herman Bartelen
発行者　松村達生
発行所　センゲージ ラーニング株式会社
　　　　〒102-0073　東京都千代田区九段北1-11-11　第2フナトビル5階
　　　　電話 03-3511-4392　FAX 03-3511-4391
　　　　e-mail: eltjapan@cengage.com
　　　　copyright©2021 センゲージ ラーニング株式会社

装　丁　　足立友幸（parastyle inc.）
制作協力　飯尾緑子（parastyle inc.）
イラスト　いなばゆみ
印刷・製本　株式会社ムレコミュニケーションズ

ISBN 978-4-86312-384-7